# The Little Encyclopedia *of Scarves*

Whether you want a little glitz or a big bold look, this versatile scarf collection offers lots of stylish choices. What a great resource it is for your crochet library!

LEISURE ARTS, INC.
Maumelle, Arkansas

## EDITORIAL STAFF

**Vice President of Publishing:** Peg Couch
**Editorial Director:** Tona Jolly
**Technical Editor:** Linda A. Daley
**Senior Graphic Artist:** Lora Puls
**Photography Technical Manager:** Stephanie Johnson
**Prepress Technician:** Janie Marie Wright
**Contributing Photographer:** Ken West
**Contributing Photo Stylist:** Sondra Daniel

## BUSINESS STAFF

**President and Chief Executive Officer:** Fred F. Pruss
**Vice President of Operations:** Donald Borin
**Vice President of Sales:** Martha Adams
**Chief Financial Officer:** Tiffany P. Childers
**Controller:** Teresa Eby
**Director of Product Development:** Lauren Binci
**Information Technology Manager:** Brian Roden
**Director of E-Commerce:** Mark Hawkins





Library of Congress Control Number: 2016938298
ISBN-13/EAN: 978-1-4647-7260-3
UPC: 0-28906-75688-3

Made in China

# Table of Contents

# Intuitive

EASY

**Finished Size:** 6" x 72" (15 cm x 183 cm)

## SHOPPING LIST

### Yarn (Fine Weight) FINE 2

[3 ounces, 498 yards
(85 grams, 455 meters) per skein]:

- ☐ 1 skein

### Crochet Hook

- ☐ Size K (6.5 mm)
  **or** size needed for gauge

### Additional Supplies

- ☐ Tapestry needle

## GAUGE INFORMATION

In pattern, 12 tr = 4" (10 cm);
4 tr rnds/rows = 5" (12.75 cm)

**Gauge Swatch:** 4" wide x 5" high
(10 cm x 12.75 cm)

Ch 15.

**Row 1:** Tr in fifth ch from hook **(4 skipped chs count as first tr)** and in each ch across: 12 tr.

**Row 2:** Ch 4 **(counts as first tr, now and throughout)**, turn; working in Back Loops Only *(Fig.1, page 92)*, tr in next tr and in each tr across.

**Row 3:** Ch 4, turn; working in Front Loops Only *(Fig.1, page 92)*, tr in next tr and in each tr across.

**Row 4:** Ch 4, turn; working in Back Loops Only, tr in next tr and in each tr across.

Finish off.

## STITCH GUIDE

### TREBLE CROCHET
*(abbreviated tr)*

YO twice, insert hook in st indicated, YO and pull up a loop (4 loops on hook), (YO and draw through 2 loops on hook) 3 times.

## SCARF

Leaving a 15" (38 cm) end for sewing, ch 37.

**Rnd 1** (Right side)**:** Sc in second ch from hook and in each ch across; join with slip st to Back Loop Only of first sc *(Fig. 1, page 92)*: 36 sc.

**Rnd 2:** Ch 1, working in Back Loops Only, sc in first 12 sc, hdc in next 12 sc, dc in last 12 sc; do **not** join, place a marker to mark the beginning of the rnd *(see Markers, page 91)*.

**Rnd 3:** Tr in Back Loop Only of each st around.

Repeat Rnd 3 for pattern until Scarf measures approximately 71" (180.5 cm) from beginning ch.

**Next Rnd:** Working in Back Loops Only, dc in next 12 tr, hdc in next 12 tr, sc in next 12 tr.

**Last Rnd:** Working in both loops, sc in each st around; join with slip st to first sc, finish off leaving a 15" (38 cm) end for sewing.

Thread tapestry needle with long end. Weave needle through sts on Last Rnd *(Fig. 6, page 93)*; draw **tightly** to close and secure end.

Repeat on opposite end, using long end from beginning ch.

*Design by Ruthie Marks.*

# Maritime

EASY

**Finished Size:** 6¼" x 61½" (16 cm x 156 cm)

*Shown on page 7.*

## SHOPPING LIST

**Yarn** (Medium Weight) MEDIUM 4

[5 ounces, 251 yards (142 grams, 230 meters) per skein]:

☐ 1 skein

**Crochet Hook**

☐ Size H (5 mm)

**or** size needed for gauge

## GAUGE INFORMATION

In pattern,

(sc, ch 5) 3 times = 4" (10 cm);

Rows 1-10 = 3⅛" (8 cm)

**Gauge Swatch:**

4¼" wide x 3⅛" high (10.75 cm x 8 cm)

Ch 20.

Work same as First Half: 4 sc, 4 Picots, and 3 ch-5 sps.

## STITCH GUIDE

**PICOT**

Ch 3, slip st in top of last sc made.

## FIRST HALF

Ch 278; place marker in second ch from hook for Second Half placement.

**Row 1** (Right side)**:** Sc in second ch from hook, ★ ch 5, skip next 5 chs, sc in next ch; repeat from ★ across: 47 sc and 46 ch-5 sps.

*Note:* Loop a short piece of yarn around any stitch to mark Row 1 as **right** side.

**Rows 2 and 3:** Ch 1, turn; sc in first sc, (ch 7, sc in next sc) across.

**Row 4:** Ch 5 (**counts as first dc plus ch 2, now and throughout**), turn; working **around** next ch-7 *(Fig. 5, page 93)*, sc in ch-7 sp one row **below**, ★ ch 5, working **around** next ch-7, sc in ch-7 sp one row **below**; repeat from ★ across to last sc, ch 2, dc in last sc: 48 sts and 47 sps.

**Row 5:** Ch 1, turn; sc in first dc, ch 2, sc in next sc, (ch 5, sc in next sc) across to last dc, ch 2, sc in last dc.

**Row 6:** Ch 5, turn; sc in next sc, (ch 7, sc in next sc) across to last sc, ch 2, dc in last sc.

**Row 7:** Ch 1, turn; sc in first dc, ch 3, sc in next sc, (ch 7, sc in next sc) across to last dc, ch 3, sc in last dc.

**Row 8:** Ch 1, turn; sc in first sc, ch 5, skip next ch-3 sp, working **around** next ch-7, sc in ch-7 sp one row **below**, ★ ch 5, working **around** next ch-7, sc in ch-7 sp one row **below**; repeat from ★ across to last ch-3 sp, ch 5, skip last ch-3 sp, sc in last sc: 47 sc and 46 ch-5 sps.

**Row 9:** Ch 1, turn; sc in first sc, (ch 5, sc in next sc) across.

**Row 10:** Ch 1, turn; sc in first sc, work Picot, ★ ch 5, sc in next sc, work Picot; repeat from ★ across; finish off.

## SECOND HALF

**Row 1:** With **right** side facing and working in free loops of beginning ch *(Fig. 2, page 92)*, join yarn with sc in first ch *(see Joining With Sc, page 91)*; ★ ch 5, skip next 5 chs, sc in next ch; repeat from ★ across ending in marked ch, remove marker: 47 sc and 46 ch-5 sps.

**Rows 2-10:** Repeat Rows 2-10 of First Half.

*Design by Ruthie Marks.*

# Roundabout

EASY +

**Finished Size:** Approximately 6¾" wide x 66¼" long (17 cm x 168.5 cm)

## SHOPPING LIST ←

### Yarn (Medium Weight) MEDIUM 4

**[**3.5 ounces, 170 yards (100 grams, 156 meters) per skein**]**:

- ☐ Color A (Bright Purple) - 1 skein
- ☐ Color B (Blue) - 1 skein
- ☐ Color C (Lt Blue) - 1 skein
- ☐ Color D (Purple) - 1 skein

### Crochet Hook

- ☐ Size I (5.5 mm) **or** size needed for gauge

## GAUGE INFORMATION

**Gauge Swatch:**

2¼" (5.75 cm) diameter

Work same as First Motif: 12 Picots.

## FIRST MOTIF

**Rnd 1** (Right side)**:** To make an adjustable loop, wind Color A around two fingers to form a ring ***(Fig. A)***, then slide yarn off fingers and grasp the strands at the top of the ring ***(Fig. B)***.

**Fig. A**

**Fig. B**

Insert hook from **front** to **back** into the ring, pull up a loop, YO and draw through loop on hook to lock the ring *(Fig. C)*, ch 6, slip st in third ch from hook **(Picot made)**, working around **both** strands, ★ dc in ring, ch 3, slip st in third ch from hook **(Picot made)**; repeat from ★ 10 times **more**, pull yarn tail to close *(Fig. D)*; join with slip st to third ch of beginning ch-6 *(Fig. E)*, finish off: 12 Picots.

**Fig. C**

**Fig. D**

**Fig. E**

*Note:* Loop a short piece of yarn around any stitch to mark Rnd 1 as **right** side.

## SECOND MOTIF

The method used to connect the Motifs is a no-sew joining known as "join-as-you-go."

Insert your hook from the **back** to the **front** through the ch-sp of any Picot on the **adjacent Motif**, keeping the working yarn at the **back** of your hook.

**Rnd 1** (Joining rnd) Make an adjustable loop with Color B *(Figs. A-C, pages 11 and 12)*, ch 6, slip st in third ch from hook **(Picot made)**, dc in ring, ★ ch 3, slip st in third ch from hook **(Picot made)**, dc in ring; repeat from ★ 9 times **more**, ch 1; holding Motifs with **right** side facing, slip st in ch-sp of any Picot on **First Motif** *(Fig. F)*, pull yarn tail to close, ch 1, slip st in next ch on **Second Motif** to form last Picot *(Fig. G)*; join with slip st to third ch of beginning ch-6, finish off: 12 Picots.

**Fig. F**

**Fig. G**

## REMAINING 80 MOTIFS

Alternating a row of 2 Motifs with a row of 3 Motifs, and using Diagram as a guide for color placement, work a Two- or Three-Side Joining to crochet Motifs together as Rnd 1 is worked. On rows containing 3 Motifs, work the center Motif first, then work the Motifs on each side of it.

**PLACEMENT DIAGRAM**

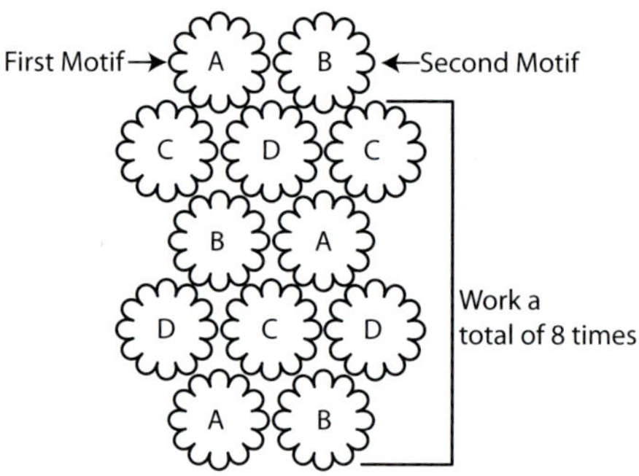


Continue inserting your hook from the **back** to the **front** through the ch-sp of Picot indicated on the **adjacent Motif**, keeping the working yarn at the **back** of your hook.

### Two-Side Joining

**Rnd 1** (Joining rnd)**:** Make an adjustable loop with next color *(Figs. A-C, pages 11 and 12)*, ch 6, slip st in third ch from hook **(Picot made)**, dc in ring, ★ ch 3, slip st in third ch from hook **(Picot made)**, dc in ring; repeat from ★ 7 times **more**, ch 1; holding Motifs with **right** side facing, skip one Picot **before** joining on **adjacent Motif** and slip st in ch-sp of next Picot (second Picot **before** joining) *(Fig. H)*, ch 1, slip st in next ch on **new Motif** to form Picot, dc in ring, ch 3, slip st in third ch from hook (**Picot made**), dc in ring, ch 1, skip joining and next Picot on **adjacent Motif** and slip st in ch-sp of next Picot (second Picot **after** joining) *(Fig. I)*, pull yarn tail to close, ch 1, slip st in next ch on **new Motif** to form last Picot; join with slip st to third ch of beginning ch-6, finish off: 12 Picots.

**Fig. H**

**Fig. I**

## Three-Side Joining

**Rnd 1** (Joining rnd)**:** Make an adjustable loop with next color *(Figs. A-C, pages 11 and 12)*, ch 6, slip st in third ch from hook (**Picot made**), dc in ring, ★ ch 3, slip st in third ch from hook (**Picot made**), dc in ring; repeat from ★ 5 times **more**, ch 1; holding Motifs with **right** side facing, skip one Picot **before** joining on **adjacent Motif** and slip st in ch-sp of next Picot (second Picot **before** joining), **[**ch 1, slip st in next ch on **new Motif** to form Picot, dc in ring, ch 3, slip st in third ch from hook (**Picot made**), dc in ring, ch 1, skip joining and next Picot on **adjacent Motif** and slip st in ch-sp of next Picot (second Picot **after** joining)**]** twice, pull yarn tail to close, ch 1, slip st in next ch on **new Motif** to form last Picot; join with slip st to third ch of beginning ch-6, finish off: 12 Picots.

*Design by Melissa Leapman.*

# Parkway

EASY

**Finished Size:** 6½" x 64½" (16.5 cm x 164 cm)

## SHOPPING LIST ⟵

### Yarn (Bulky Weight) BULKY 5

[4 ounces, 86 yards
(113 grams, 78 meters) per skein]:

☐ 2 skeins

### Crochet Hook

☐ Size L (8 mm)
**or** size needed for gauge

---

## GAUGE INFORMATION

In pattern, 9 sc = 4" (10 cm);
Rows 1-5 = 3¼" (8.25 cm)

**Gauge Swatch:**
5¾" wide x 3¼" high
(14.5 cm x 8.25 cm)

Ch 14.

Work same as First Half: 15 sts.

## FIRST HALF

Ch 146; place marker in second ch from hook for Second Half placement.

**Row 1** (Right side)**:** Sc in second ch from hook and in each ch across: 145 sc.

*Note:* Loop a short piece of yarn around any stitch to mark Row 1 as **right** side.

**Rows 2 and 3:** Ch 1, turn; sc in each sc across.

**Row 4:** Ch 3 **(counts as first dc)**, turn; skip next 2 sc, 5 dc in next sc, ★ ch 1, skip next 5 sc, 5 dc in next sc; repeat from ★ across to last 3 sc, skip next 2 sc, dc in last sc: 122 dc and 23 ch-1 sps.

**Row 5:** Ch 1, turn; sc in first dc, skip next 2 dc, 6 dc in next dc, ★ sc in next ch-1 sp, skip next 2 dc, 6 dc in next dc; repeat from ★ across to last 3 dc, skip next 2 dc, sc in last dc; finish off.

## SECOND HALF

**Row 1:** With **right** side facing and working in free loops of beginning ch *(Fig. 2, page 92)*, join yarn with sc in first ch *(see Joining With Sc, page 91)*; sc in next ch and in each ch across ending in marked ch, remove marker: 145 sc.

**Rows 2-5:** Repeat Rows 2-5 of First Half.

*Design by Ruthie Marks.*

# Basketweave

**INTERMEDIATE**

**Finished Size:** 5½" x 56" (14 cm x 142 cm)

*Shown on page 19.*

## SHOPPING LIST

### Yarn (Medium Weight) MEDIUM 4

[3.5 ounces, 207 yards (100 grams, 188 meters) per skein]:

- ☐ Brown - 3 skeins
- ☐ Dk Grey - 1 skein
- ☐ Cream - 1 skein

### Crochet Hook

- ☐ Size I (5.5 mm) **or** size needed for gauge

## GAUGE INFORMATION

In Basketweave pattern,
12 sts = 3" (7.5 cm);
12 rows = 4¼" (10.75 cm)

**Gauge Swatch:**
3½" (9 cm) square

Work same as Basketweave pattern for 9 rows: 14 sts.

## STITCH GUIDE

**FRONT POST DOUBLE CROCHET** *(abbreviated FPdc)*

YO, insert hook from **front** to **back** around post of st indicated *(Fig. 4, page 93)*, YO and pull up a loop (3 loops on hook), (YO and draw through 2 loops on hook) twice.

**BACK POST DOUBLE CROCHET** *(abbreviated BPdc)*

YO, insert hook from **back** to **front** around post of st indicated *(Fig. 4, page 93)*, YO and pull up a loop (3 loops on hook), (YO and draw through 2 loops on hook) twice.

## BASKETWEAVE PATTERN

With Brown, ch 16.

**Row 1** (Right side)**:** Dc in fourth ch from hook **(3 skipped chs count as first dc)** and in each ch across: 14 dc.

*Note:* Loop a short piece of yarn around any stitch to mark Row 1 as **right** side and bottom edge.

**Rows 2 and 3:** Ch 3 **(counts as first dc, now and throughout)**, turn; ★ work FPdc around each of next 3 sts, work BPdc around each of next 3 sts; repeat from ★ once **more**, dc in last dc.

**Rows 4-6:** Ch 3, turn; ★ work BPdc around each of next 3 sts, work FPdc around each of next 3 sts; repeat from ★ once **more**, dc in last dc.

**Rows 7-9:** Ch 3, turn; ★ work FPdc around each of next 3 sts, work BPdc around each of next 3 sts; repeat from ★ once **more**, dc in last dc.

Repeat Rows 4-9 for pattern until piece measures approximately 55¾" (141.5 cm) from beginning ch, ending by working Row 8.

Finish off.

## EDGING

For Row 2 to work, you will need an odd number of stitches on Row 1, but that number also needs to be a multiple of 6 plus 1 in order for Row 1 of the Twisted Cable Trim to work.

On Row 1, work sc across making sure that the scarf lays flat. When you get near the end, count your stitches in groups of 6, ending with one extra stitch. Complete the row, adjusting the number as needed in order for your total number of sc to be the correct multiple.

**Row 1:** With **right** side facing and working in end of rows, join Dk Grey with sc in first row *(see Joining With Sc, page 91)*; sc evenly across working a total number of sts that is a multiple of 6 plus 1.

**Row 2:** Ch 1, turn; sc in first sc, ★ ch 1, skip next sc, sc in next sc; repeat from ★ across; finish off.

**Row 3:** With **right** side facing, join Cream with sc in first sc; sc in next ch-1 sp, (ch 1, sc in next ch-1 sp) across to last sc, sc in last sc.

**Row 4:** Ch 1, turn; sc in first sc and in each sc and each ch-1 sp across; finish off.

Repeat Edging on second side.

## TWISTED CABLE TRIM

**Rnd 1:** With **right** side facing and beginning at bottom edge, join Brown with sc in first sc on Row 4 of Edging; ch 1, sc in same st, ch 3, (skip next 2 sc, sc in next sc, ch 3) across to last 3 sc, skip next 2 sc, (sc, ch 1, sc) in last sc; sc evenly across end of rows on Edgings and in each st on last row of Basketweave Pattern; working across Row 4 of Edging, (sc, ch 1, sc) in first sc, ch 3, (skip next 2 sc, sc in next sc, ch 3) across to last 3 sc, skip next 2 sc, (sc, ch 1, sc) in last sc; sc evenly across end of rows on Edgings and in free loops of chs on Basketweave Pattern *(Fig. 2, page 92)*; join with slip st to first sc, finish off.

**First Side:** With **right** side facing, join Dk Grey with sc in corner ch-1 sp; ch 3, ★ remove hook from loop, insert hook from **front** to **back** through next ch-3 sp, hook loop and draw through sp, ch 3; repeat from ★ across, sc in corner ch-1 sp; finish off.

Repeat for second side.

*Design by Mary Estok Nolfi.*

# Confidence

INTERMEDIATE

**Finished Size:** 4¼" x 56½" (11 cm x 143.5 cm)

## SHOPPING LIST ←

### Yarn (Medium Weight) MEDIUM 4

**[**3.5 ounces, 170 yards (100 grams, 156 meters) per skein**]**:

- ☐ 2 skeins

### Crochet Hook

- ☐ Size L (8 mm) **or** size needed for gauge

## GAUGE INFORMATION

In pattern,

10 lqtr = 4" (10 cm);

one lqtr row = 2¼" (5.75 cm)

**Gauge Swatch:**

4" wide x 3" high (10 cm x 7.5 cm)

Ch 11.

Work same as First Half, page 27: 10 lqtr.

## STITCH GUIDE

### BEGINNING LINKED QUADRUPLE TREBLE CROCHET

*(abbreviated beginning lqtr)*

Ch 6, turn; pull up a loop in second ch from hook and in next 4 chs (6 loops on hook), insert hook in first sc, YO and pull up a loop (7 loops on hook), (YO and draw through 2 loops on hook) 6 times.

### LINKED QUADRUPLE TREBLE CROCHET *(abbreviated lqtr)*

Skip top loops of last st made, ★ insert hook in next horizontal bar *(Fig. A)*, YO and pull up a loop; repeat from ★ 4 times **more** (6 loops on hook), insert hook in next sc, YO and pull up a loop (7 loops on hook), (YO and draw through 2 loops on hook) 6 times.

**Fig. A**

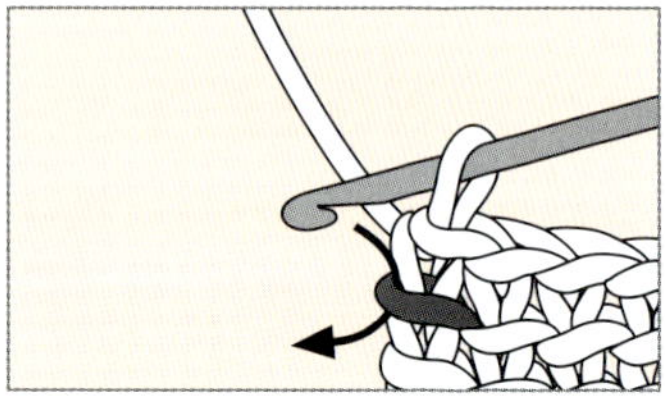

### CLUSTER (uses one st)

★ YO, insert hook in st indicated, YO and pull up a loop, YO and draw through 2 loops on hook; repeat from ★ 3 times **more**, YO and draw through all 5 loops on hook. Push Cluster to **right** side.

## FIRST HALF

Ch 136; place marker in second ch from hook for Second Half placement.

**Row 1** (Right side): Sc in second ch from hook and in each ch across: 135 sc.

*Note:* Loop a short piece of yarn around any stitch to mark Row 1 as **right** side.

**Row 2:** Ch 1, turn; sc in each sc across.

**Row 3:** Work beginning lqtr, work lqtr across; finish off.

## SECOND HALF

**Row 1:** With **right** side facing and working in free loops of beginning ch *(Fig. 2, page 92)*, join yarn with sc in first ch *(see Joining With Sc, page 91)*; sc in each ch across ending in marked ch, remove marker: 135 sc.

**Row 2:** Ch 1, turn; sc in first 3 sc, (work Cluster in next sc, sc in next 3 sc) across.

**Row 3:** Ch 1, turn; sc in each st across; do **not** finish off.

## EDGING

**Rnd 1:** Ch 1, do **not** turn; sc evenly across ends of rows; 3 sc in first lqtr, sc in each lqtr across to last lqtr, 3 sc in last lqtr; sc evenly across ends of rows; 3 sc in first sc, sc in each sc across to last sc, 3 sc in last sc; join with slip st to first sc.

**Rnd 2:** Slip st in each st around; join with slip st to first slip st, finish off.

*Design by Ruthie Marks.*

# Dynamic

EASY +

**Finished Size:** 4½" x 59" (11.5 cm x 150 cm) excluding fringe

## SHOPPING LIST

### Yarn (Medium Weight) MEDIUM 4

**[**3.5 ounces, 205 yards (100 grams, 187 meters) per skein**]**:

- ☐ Orange - 1 skein
- ☐ Gold - 1 skein
- ☐ Burgundy - 1 skein

### Crochet Hook

- ☐ Size G (4 mm)
  **or** size needed for gauge

## GAUGE INFORMATION

In pattern,
5 Clusters = 4½" (11.5 cm);
Rows 1-7 = 4" (10 cm)

**Gauge Swatch:**
4½" wide x 4" high
(11.5 cm x 10 cm)

Work same as Scarf through Row 7: 6 sc and 5 Clusters.

## STITCH GUIDE

**CLUSTER** (uses one st)

Ch 3, ★ YO, insert hook in same st as last sc made, YO and pull up a loop, YO and draw through 2 loops on hook; repeat from ★ 4 times **more**, YO and draw through all 6 loops on hook.

## BODY

With Orange, ch 22.

**Row 1** (Wrong side)**:** Sc in second ch from hook, ★ work Cluster, skip next 3 chs, sc in next ch; repeat from ★ across changing to Gold in last sc made ***(Fig. 3a, page 92)***; cut Orange: 6 sc and 5 Clusters.

***Note:*** Loop a short piece of yarn around the **back** of any stitch on Row 1 to mark **right** side.

**Row 2:** Ch 6 (**counts as first dc plus ch 3, now and throughout**), turn; skip next Cluster, dc in next sc, ★ ch 3, skip next Cluster, dc in next sc; repeat from ★ across: 6 dc and 5 ch-3 sps.

**Row 3:** Ch 1, turn; sc in first dc, ★ work Cluster, skip next ch-3 sp, sc in next dc; repeat from ★ across changing to Orange in last sc made; cut Gold: 6 sc and 5 Clusters.

**Row 4:** Ch 6, turn; skip next Cluster, dc in next sc, ★ ch 3, skip next Cluster, dc in next sc; repeat from ★ across: 6 dc and 5 ch-3 sps.

**Row 5:** Repeat Row 3 changing to Burgundy in last sc made; cut Orange: 6 sc and 5 Clusters.

**Row 6:** Ch 6, turn; skip next Cluster, dc in next sc, ★ ch 3, skip next Cluster, dc in next sc; repeat from ★ across: 6 dc and 5 ch-3 sps.

**Row 7:** Repeat Row 3; cut Burgundy: 6 sc and 5 Clusters.

**Row 8:** Ch 6, turn; skip next Cluster, dc in next sc, ★ ch 3, skip next Cluster, dc in next sc; repeat from ★ across: 6 dc and 5 ch-3 sps.

**Row 9:** Repeat Row 3 changing to Gold in last sc made; cut Orange: 6 sc and 5 Clusters.

**Rows 10-104:** Repeat Rows 2-9, 11 times; then repeat Rows 2-8 once **more**: 6 dc and 5 ch-3 sps.

**Row 105:** Ch 1, turn; sc in first dc, ★ work Cluster, skip next ch-3 sp, sc in next dc; repeat from ★ across; finish off: 6 sc and 5 Clusters.

## FRINGE

### First End

**First Fringe:** With **right** side facing, join Gold with slip st in first sc on Row 105; ch 6, skip next Cluster, dc in next sc, ch 1, **turn**; sc in dc just made, work Cluster, skip next 3 chs, sc in next ch, ch 6, **turn**; skip next Cluster, dc in last sc made, ch 1, **turn**; sc in dc just made, work Cluster, skip next 3 chs, slip st in next ch; finish off.

**Next Two Fringes:** With **right** side facing, skip next Cluster on Row 105 and join Gold with slip st in next sc; complete same as First Fringe.

### Second End

**First Fringe:** With **right** side facing and working in free loops of beginning ch *(Fig. 2, page 92)*, join Burgundy with slip st in ch at base of first sc; ch 6, skip next Cluster, dc in next sc, ch 1, **turn**; sc in dc just made, work Cluster, skip next 3 chs, sc in next ch, ch 6, **turn**; skip next Cluster, dc in last sc made, ch 1, **turn**; sc in dc just made, work Cluster, skip next 3 chs, slip st in next ch; finish off.

**Next Two Fringes:** With **right** side facing, skip next 3 chs on beginning ch and join Burgundy with slip st in next ch; complete same as First Fringe.

*Design by Ruthie Marks.*

# Simplicity

EASY

**Finished Size:** 4" x 69" (10 cm x 175.5 cm)

## SHOPPING LIST

### Yarn (Medium Weight) MEDIUM 4

**[**2 ounces, 95 yards

(57 grams, 86 meters) per skein**]**:

- ☐ 3 skeins

### Crochet Hook

- ☐ Size I (5.5 mm)
  **or** size needed for gauge

## GAUGE INFORMATION

In pattern, 16 sts = 4" (10 cm);
8 rows = 3½" (9 cm)

**Gauge Swatch:**
4" wide x 3½" high
(10 cm x 9 cm)

Work same as Body for 8 rows: 16 sts.

## BODY

Ch 17.

**Row 1** (Right side)**:** Hdc in second ch from hook and in each ch across: 16 hdc.

*Note:* Loop a short piece of yarn around any stitch to mark Row 1 as **right** side.

**Row 2:** Ch 1, turn; slip st in Back Loop Only *(Fig. 1, page 92)* of first hdc and each hdc across.

**Row 3:** Ch 2 **(does not count as a st)**, turn; hdc in Front Loop Only *(Fig. 1, pag 92)* of first slip st and each slip st across.

Repeat Rows 2 and 3 for pattern until Body measures approximately 65½" (166.5 cm) from beginning ch, ending by working Row 3.

Finish off.

## First End

**Row 1** (Right side)**:** With **right** side facing and working in both loops of hdc on last row, join yarn with sc in first hdc ***(see Joining With Sc, page 91)***; ch 6, skip next 6 hdc, sc in next 2 hdc, ch 6, skip next 6 hdc, sc in last hdc: 4 sc and 2 ch-6 sps.

**Row 2:** Ch 1, turn; sc in first sc, 6 sc in next ch-6 sp, sc in next 2 sc, 6 sc in next ch-6 sp, sc in last sc: 16 sc.

**Row 3:** Ch 1, turn; sc in first 2 sc, hdc in next sc, dc in next sc, ch 3, dc in next sc, hdc in next sc, sc in next 4 sc, hdc in next sc, dc in next sc, ch 3, dc in next sc, hdc in next sc, sc in last 2 sc; finish off.

## Second End

**Row 1:** With **right** side facing and working in free loops of beginning ch ***(Fig. 2, page 92)***, join yarn with sc in first ch; ch 6, skip next 6 chs, sc in next 2 chs, ch 6, skip next 6 chs, sc in next 2 chs: 4 sc and 2 ch-6 sps.

**Rows 2 and 3:** Work same as First End.

*Design by Ruthie Marks.*

# Filigree

EASY

**Finished Size:** 7½" x 64½" (19 cm x 164 cm)

*Shown on page 35.*

## SHOPPING LIST

**Yarn** (Super Bulky Weight) SUPER BULKY 6

[3.5 ounces, 108 yards (100 grams, 99 meters) per skein]:

- ☐ 2 skeins

**Crochet Hook**

- ☐ Size L (8 mm) **or** size needed for gauge

## GAUGE INFORMATION

In pattern, 9 sc = 4" (10 cm);
Rows 1-5 = 3¾" (9.5 cm)

**Gauge Swatch:**
4½" wide x 3¾" high
(11.5 cm x 9.5 cm)

Ch 11.

Work same as First Half: 10 sc and 3 Picots.

## STITCH GUIDE

**PICOT**

Ch 3, slip st in top of last sc made.

## FIRST HALF

Ch 146; place marker in second ch from hook for Second Half placement.

**Row 1:** Sc in second ch from hook and in each ch across: 145 sc.

**Row 2** (Right side)**:** Ch 5 **(counts as first dc plus ch 2, now and throughout)**, turn; skip next 2 sc, dc in next sc, ★ ch 2, skip next 2 sc, dc in next sc; repeat from ★ across: 49 dc and 48 ch-2 sps.

*Note:* Loop a short piece of yarn around any stitch to mark Row 2 as **right** side.

**Row 3:** Ch 1, turn; sc in first dc, ★ (sc, work Picot, sc) in next ch-2 sp, sc in next dc; repeat from ★ across: 145 sc and 48 Picots.

**Row 4:** Ch 5, turn; skip next Picot and next sc, dc in next sc, ★ ch 2, skip next Picot and next sc, dc in next sc; repeat from ★ across: 49 dc and 48 ch-2 sps.

**Row 5:** Ch 1, turn; sc in first dc, ★ (sc, work Picot, sc) in next ch-2 sp, sc in next dc; repeat from ★ across; finish off.

## SECOND HALF

**Row 1:** With **wrong** side facing and working in free loops of beginning ch ***(Fig. 2, page 92)***, join yarn with sc in first ch ***(see Joining With Sc, page 91)***; sc in next ch and in each ch across ending in marked ch, remove marker: 145 sc.

**Rows 2-5:** Repeat Rows 2-5 of First Half.

*Design by Ruthie Marks.*

# Checkmate

**EASY +**

**Finished Size:** 6½" x 61" (16.5 cm x 155 cm) excluding fringe

## SHOPPING LIST

### Yarn (Medium Weight) 4

[3.5 ounces, 170 yards (100 grams, 156 meters) per skein]:

- ☐ Purple - 1 skein
- ☐ Lt Purple - 1 skein

### Crochet Hook

- ☐ Size J (6 mm) **or** size needed for gauge

## GAUGE INFORMATION

In pattern, 7 sts = 2½" (6.25 cm);

Rows 1-12 = 6½" (16.5 cm)

**Gauge Swatch:**

6½" (16.5 cm) square

Work same as Body through Row 12: 18 sc.

## STITCH GUIDE

**CLUSTER** (uses one dc)

★ YO, insert hook in dc indicated, YO and pull up a loop, YO and draw through 2 loops on hook; repeat from ★ 2 times **more**, YO and draw through all 4 loops on hook. Push Cluster to **right** side.

## BODY

With Purple, ch 9, do **not** cut Purple; with Lt Purple, ch 11: 20 chs.

**Row 1:** Dc in fourth ch from hook **(3 skipped chs count as first dc)** and in next 7 chs changing to Purple in last dc made *(Fig. 3c, page 92)*, drop Lt Purple to front (**wrong** side); with Purple, dc in last 9 chs: 18 dc.

Always drop unused yarn to **wrong** side of piece in same manner. Do **not** cut yarn until instructed.

**Row 2** (Right side)**:** Ch 4 **(counts as first dc plus ch 1, now and throughout)**, turn; skip next dc, (dc in next dc, ch 1, skip next dc) 3 times, dc in next dc changing to Lt Purple; dc in next dc, (ch 1, skip next dc, dc in next dc) 4 times: 10 dc and 8 ch-1 sps.

*Note:* Loop a short piece of yarn around any stitch to mark Row 2 as **right** side.

**Row 3:** Ch 1, turn; sc in first dc and in next ch-1 sp, (work Cluster in next dc, sc in next ch-1 sp) 3 times, sc in next dc changing to Purple *(Fig. 3b, page 92)*; sc in next dc and in next ch-1 sp, (work Cluster in next dc, sc in next ch-1 sp) 3 times, sc in last dc: 12 sc and 6 Clusters.

**Row 4:** Ch 1, turn; sc in first 9 sts changing to Lt Purple in last sc made; sc in last 9 sts: 18 sc.

**Row 5:** Ch 3 **(counts as first dc, now and throughout)**, turn; dc in next 8 sc changing to Purple in last dc made; dc in last 9 sc.

**Row 6:** Ch 4, turn; skip next dc, (dc in next dc, ch 1, skip next dc) 3 times, dc in next dc changing to Lt Purple; dc in next dc, (ch 1, skip next dc, dc in next dc) 4 times: 10 dc and 8 ch-1 sps.

**Rows 7-15:** Repeat Rows 3-6 twice, then repeat Row 3 once **more**: 12 sc and 6 Clusters.

**Row 16:** Ch 1, turn; sc in first 9 sts changing to Lt Purple in last sc made, cut Purple; sc in last 9 sts changing to Purple in last sc *(Fig. 3a, page 92)*, cut Lt Purple: 18 sc.

**Row 17:** Ch 3, turn; dc in next 8 sc changing to Lt Purple in last dc made; dc in last 9 sc.

**Row 18:** Ch 4, turn; skip next dc, (dc in next dc, ch 1, skip next dc) 3 times, dc in next dc changing to Purple; dc in next dc, (ch 1, skip next dc, dc in next dc) 4 times: 10 dc and 8 ch-1 sps.

**Row 19:** Ch 1, turn; sc in first dc and in next ch-1 sp, (work Cluster in next dc, sc in next ch-1 sp) 3 times, sc in next dc changing to Lt Purple; sc in next dc and in next ch-1 sp, (work Cluster in next dc, sc in next ch-1 sp) 3 times, sc in last dc: 12 sc and 6 Clusters.

**Row 20:** Ch 1, turn; sc in first 9 sts changing to Purple in last sc made; sc in last 9 sts: 18 sc.

**Rows 21-27:** Repeat Rows 17-20 once, then repeat Rows 17-19 once **more**: 12 sc and 6 Clusters.

**Row 28:** Ch 1, turn; sc in first 9 sts changing to Purple in last sc made, cut Lt Purple; sc in last 9 sts changing to Lt Purple in last sc, cut Purple: 18 sc.

**Row 29:** Ch 3, turn; dc in next 8 sc changing to Purple in last dc made; dc in last 9 sc.

**Row 30:** Ch 4, turn; skip next dc, (dc in next dc, ch 1, skip next dc) 3 times, dc in next dc changing to Lt Purple; dc in next dc, (ch 1, skip next dc, dc in next dc) 4 times: 10 dc and 8 ch-1 sps.

**Rows 31-111:** Repeat Rows 3-30 twice, then repeat Rows 3-27 once **more**: 12 sc and 6 Clusters.

**Row 112:** Ch 1, turn; sc in first 9 sts changing to Purple in last sc made, cut Lt Purple; sc in last 9 sts; finish off.

## FRINGE

Holding 3 strands of yarn together, each 8" (20.5 cm) long, add fringe, having 5 fringes of opposite color yarn across each color section *(Figs. 7a & b, page 94)*.

*Design by Ruthie Marks.*

# Collegiate

EASY +

**Finished Size:** 6" x 71" (15 cm x 180.5 cm)

*Shown on page 43.*

## SHOPPING LIST

### Yarn (Light Weight) LIGHT 3

**[**2.2 ounces,102 yards (65 grams, 93 meters) per ball**]**:

- ☐ Plum - 3 balls
- ☐ Gold - 3 balls

### Crochet Hook

- ☐ Size G (4 mm) **or** size needed for gauge

## GAUGE INFORMATION

In pattern, 16 sc = 4" (10 cm); Rows 1-14 = 4½" (11.5 cm)

**Gauge Swatch:** 4" (10 cm) square

With Plum, ch 17.

**Row 1:** Sc in second ch from hook and in each ch across: 16 sc.

**Rows 2-16:** Ch 1, turn; sc in each sc across.

Finish off.

## STITCH GUIDE

**CLUSTER** (uses one sc)

★ YO, insert hook in sc indicated, YO and pull up a loop, YO and draw through 2 loops on hook; repeat from ★ once **more**, YO and draw through all 3 loops on hook **(counts as one dc)**.

**DOUBLE CROCHET 2 TOGETHER *(abbreviated dc2tog)*** (uses 2 sts)

YO, insert hook in same st as dc just made, YO and pull up a loop, YO and draw through 2 loops on hook, YO, insert hook in turning ch-1 **or** in last sc, YO and pull up a loop, YO and draw through 2 loops on hook, cut yarn; with color indicated, YO and draw through all 3 loops on hook **(counts as one dc)**.

## SCARF

With Plum, ch 25.

**Row 1:** Sc in second ch from hook and in each ch across: 24 sc.

**Rows 2-4:** Ch 1, turn; sc in each sc across.

**Row 5:** Ch 1, turn; sc in each sc across changing to Gold in last sc *(Fig. 3a, page 92)*; cut Plum.

**Row 6:** Ch 3 **(counts as first dc, now and throughout)**, turn; skip next sc, (dc, ch 1, Cluster) in next sc, ★ skip next 2 sc, (dc, ch 1, Cluster) in next sc; repeat from ★ across to last 3 sc, skip next 2 sc, dc in last sc, ch 1, dc2tog changing to Plum *(Fig. 3c, page 92)*; cut Gold: 17 dc and 8 ch-1 sps.

**Row 7:** Ch 1, turn; sc in each dc and in each ch-1 sp across to last 2 dc, skip next dc, sc in last dc changing to Gold; cut Plum: 24 sc.

**Row 8:** Ch 4 **(counts as first dc plus ch 1)**, turn; work Cluster in next sc, ★ skip next 2 sc, (dc, ch 1, Cluster) in next sc; repeat from ★ across to last 4 sc, skip next 2 sc, dc in next sc, ch 1, dc2tog changing to Plum; cut Gold: 16 dc and 8 ch-1 sps.

**Row 9:** Ch 1, turn; sc in each st and in each ch-1 sp across changing to Gold in last sc; cut Plum: 24 sc.

**Row 10:** Ch 3, turn; work Cluster in first sc, ★ skip next 2 sc, (dc, ch 1, Cluster) in next sc; repeat from ★ across to last 2 sc, skip next sc, dc in last sc changing to Plum; cut Gold: 17 dc and 7 ch-1 sps.

**Row 11:** Ch 1, turn; sc in each dc and in each ch-1 sp across: 24 sc.

**Rows 12-14:** Ch 1, turn; sc in each sc across.

**Row 15:** Ch 1, turn; sc in each sc across changing to Gold in last sc; cut Plum.

**Rows 16-25:** Repeat Rows 6-15.

**Rows 26-28:** Ch 1, turn; sc in each sc across.

**Row 29:** Ch 1, turn; sc in each sc across changing to Plum in last sc; cut Gold.

**Row 30:** Ch 3, turn; skip next sc, (dc, ch 1, Cluster) in next sc, ★ skip next 2 sc, (dc, ch 1, Cluster) in next sc; repeat from ★ across to last 3 sc, skip next 2 sc, dc in last sc, ch 1, dc2tog changing to Gold; cut Plum: 17 dc and 8 ch-1 sps.

**Row 31:** Ch 1, turn; sc in each dc and each ch-1 sp across to last 2 dc, skip next dc, sc in last dc changing to Plum; cut Gold: 24 sc.

**Row 32:** Ch 3, turn; skip next sc, (dc, ch 1, Cluster) in next sc, ★ skip next 2 sc, (dc, ch 1, Cluster) in next sc; repeat from ★ across to last 3 sc, skip next 2 sc, dc in last sc, ch 1, dc2tog changing to Gold; cut Plum: 17 dc and 8 ch-1 sps.

**Row 33:** Ch 1, turn; sc in each dc and each ch-1 sp across to last 2 dc, skip next dc, sc in last dc changing to Plum; cut Gold: 24 sc.

**Row 34:** Ch 3, turn; work Cluster in first sc, ★ skip next 2 sc, (dc, ch 1, Cluster) in next sc; repeat from ★ across to last 2 sc, skip next sc, dc in last sc changing to Gold; cut Plum: 17 dc and 7 ch-1 sps.

**Row 35:** Ch 1, turn; sc in each dc and in each ch-1 sp across: 24 sc.

**Rows 36 and 37:** Ch 1, turn; sc in each sc across.

**Row 38:** Ch 1, turn; sc in each sc across changing to Plum in last sc; cut Gold.

**Row 39:** Ch 1, turn; sc in each sc across.

**Rows 40-214:** Repeat Rows 2-39, 4 times; then repeat Rows 2-24 once **more**.

**Row 215:** Ch 1, turn; sc in each sc across; finish off.

*Design by Ruthie Marks.*

# Keyhole Ascot

EASY +

**Finished Size:** 6½" x 33" (16.5 cm x 84 cm)

## SHOPPING LIST

### Yarn (Medium Weight)

[2.5 ounces, 175 yards

(70 grams, 160 meters) per skein]:

- ☐ Variegated - 1 skein

### Crochet Hook

- ☐ Size K (6.5 mm)

  **or** size needed for gauge

### Additional Supplies

- ☐ Safety pin

---

## GAUGE INFORMATION

In pattern,

(sc, ch 1) 4 times = 2" (5 cm);

5 rows = 1½" (3.75 cm)

**Gauge Swatch:**

6½" wide x 4" high

(16.5 cm x 10 cm)

Work same as Ascot, page 50, through Row 12: 14 sc and 11 ch-1 sps.

## STITCH GUIDE

**BEGINNING SINGLE CROCHET 2 TOGETHER**

*(abbreviated beginning sc2tog)*

(uses first sc and next ch-1 sp)

Pull up a loop in first sc and in next ch-1 sp, YO and draw through all 3 loops on hook **(counts as one sc)**.

**ENDING SINGLE CROCHET 2 TOGETHER**

*(abbreviated ending sc2tog)*

(uses last ch-1 sp and last sc)

Pull up a loop in last ch-1 sp and in last sc, YO and draw through all 3 loops on hook **(counts as one sc)**.

## ASCOT

To make the opening in the Ascot, Rows 23-28 are worked in two separate parts. Before beginning the Ascot, wind 5 yards (4.5 meters) into a ball to use for the Second Part of Rows 23-28.

**Row 1** (Right side)**:** Ch 2, 3 sc in second ch from hook: 3 sc.

*Note:* Loop a short piece of yarn around any stitch to mark Row 1 as **right** side.

**Row 2:** Ch 1, turn; 2 sc in first sc, ch 1, skip next sc, 2 sc in last sc: 4 sc and one ch-1 sp.

**Row 3:** Ch 1, turn; 2 sc in first sc, ch 1, skip next sc, sc in next ch-1 sp, ch 1, skip next sc, 2 sc in last sc: 5 sc and 2 ch-1 sps.

**Rows 4-13** (Increase rows)**:** Ch 1, turn; 2 sc in first sc, ch 1, ★ skip next sc, sc in next ch-1 sp, ch 1; repeat from ★ across to last 2 sc, skip next sc, 2 sc in last sc: 15 sc and 12 ch-1 sps.

**Row 14:** Ch 1, turn; sc in first sc, ch 1, ★ skip next sc, sc in next ch-1 sp, ch 1; repeat from ★ across to last 2 sc, skip next sc, sc in last sc: 14 sc and 13 ch-1 sps.

**Rows 15-22** (Decrease rows)**:** Ch 1, turn; work beginning sc2tog, ch 1, skip next sc, ★ sc in next ch-1 sp, ch 1, skip next sc; repeat from ★ across to last ch-1 sp, work ending sc2tog: 6 sc and 5 ch-1 sps.

**Row 23 - First Part:** Ch 1, turn; sc in first sc and in next ch-1 sp, ch 1, skip next sc, sc in next ch-1 sp and in next sc, leave remaining 3 sc and 3 ch-1 sps unworked: 4 sc and one ch-1 sp.

**Row 24 - First Part:** Ch 1, turn; sc in first sc, ch 1, skip next sc, sc in next ch-1 sp, ch 1, skip next sc, sc in last sc: 3 sc and 2 ch-1 sps.

**Row 25 - First Part:** Ch 1, turn; sc in first sc and in next ch-1 sp, ch 1, skip next sc, sc in next ch-1 sp and in last sc: 4 sc and one ch-1 sp.

**Rows 26 thru 28 - First Part:** Repeat Rows 24 and 25 once, then repeat Row 24 once **more**.

Do **not** finish off. Slip loop from hook onto safety pin to keep the piece from unraveling so that you may work Second Part.

**Row 23 - Second Part:** With **right** side facing, skip first unworked ch-1 sp on Row 22 and join yarn from small ball with sc in next unworked sc ***(see Joining With Sc, page 91)***; sc in next ch-1 sp, ch 1, skip next sc, sc in next ch-1 sp and in last sc: 4 sc and one ch-1 sp.

**Row 24 - Second Part:** Ch 1, turn; sc in first sc, ch 1, skip next sc, sc in next ch-1 sp, ch 1, skip next sc, sc in last sc: 3 sc and 2 ch-1 sps.

**Row 25 - Second Part:** Ch 1, turn; sc in first sc and in next ch-1 sp, ch 1, skip next sc, sc in next ch-1 sp and in last sc: 4 sc and one ch-1 sp.

**Rows 26 thru 28 - Second Part:** Repeat Rows 24 and 25 once, then repeat Row 24 once **more**.

Finish off.

**Row 29** (Joining row)**:** With **right** side facing, slip loop from safety pin onto hook; ch 1, sc in first sc and in next ch-1 sp, ch 1, skip next sc, sc in next ch-1 sp and in next sc, ch 1, sc in first sc on Second Part and in next ch-1 sp, ch 1, skip next sc, sc in next ch-1 sp and in last sc: 8 sc and 3 ch-1 sps.

**Row 30** (Increase row)**:** Ch 1, turn; 2 sc in first sc, ch 1, skip next sc, sc in next ch-1 sp, ch 1, skip next sc, sc in next sc, ch 1, skip next ch-1 sp, sc in next sc, ch 1, skip next sc, sc in next ch-1 sp, ch 1, skip next sc, 2 sc in last sc: 8 sc and 5 ch-1 sps.

**Rows 31-37** (Increase rows)**:** Ch 1, turn; 2 sc in first sc, ch 1, (skip next sc, sc in next ch-1 sp, ch 1) across to last 2 sc, skip next sc, 2 sc in last sc: 15 sc and 12 ch-1 sps.

**Row 38:** Ch 1, turn; sc in first sc, ch 1, ★ skip next sc, sc in next ch-1 sp, ch 1; repeat from ★ across to last 2 sc, skip next sc, sc in last sc: 14 sc and 13 ch-1 sps.

**Row 39:** Ch 1, turn; sc in first sc and in next ch-1 sp, ★ ch 1, skip next sc, sc in next ch-1 sp; repeat from ★ across to last sc, sc in last sc: 15 sc and 12 ch-1 sps.

**Rows 40-72:** Repeat Rows 38 and 39, 16 times; then repeat Row 38 once **more**: 14 sc and 13 ch-1 sps.

**Rows 73-80** (Decrease rows)**:** Ch 1, turn; work beginning sc2tog, ch 1, skip next sc, ★ sc in next ch-1 sp, ch 1, skip next sc; repeat from ★ across to last ch-1 sp, work ending sc2tog: 6 sc and 5 ch-1 sps.

**Row 81:** Ch 1, turn; sc in first sc and in next ch-1 sp, ★ ch 1, skip next sc, sc in next ch-1 sp; repeat from ★ across to last sc, sc in last sc: 7 sc and 4 ch-1 sps.

**Row 82:** Ch 1, turn; sc in first sc, ch 1, ★ skip next sc, sc in next ch-1 sp, ch 1; repeat from ★ across to last 2 sc, skip next sc, sc in last sc: 6 sc and 5 ch-1 sps.

**Rows 83-87:** Repeat Rows 81 and 82 twice, then repeat Row 81 once **more**: 7 sc and 4 ch-1 sps.

**Rows 88-95** (Increase rows)**:** Ch 1, turn; 2 sc in first sc, ch 1, ★ skip next sc, sc in next ch-1 sp, ch 1; repeat from ★ across to last 2 sc, skip next sc, 2 sc in last sc: 15 sc and 12 ch-1 sps.

**Row 96:** Ch 1, turn; sc in first sc, ch 1, ★ skip next sc, sc in next ch-1 sp, ch 1; repeat from ★ across to last 2 sc, skip next sc, sc in last sc: 14 sc and 13 ch-1 sps.

**Rows 97-106** (Decrease rows)**:** Ch 1, turn; work beginning sc2tog, ch 1, skip next sc, ★ sc in next ch-1 sp, ch 1, skip next sc; repeat from ★ across to last ch-1 sp, work ending sc2tog: 4 sc and 3 ch-1 sps.

**Row 107:** Ch 1, turn; work beginning sc2tog, ch 1, skip next sc, sc in next ch-1 sp, ch 1, skip next sc, work ending sc2tog: 3 sc and 2 ch-1 sps.

**Row 108:** Ch 1, turn; work beginning sc2tog, ch 1, skip next sc, work ending sc2tog: 2 sc and one ch-1 sp.

**Row 109:** Ch 1, turn; pull up a loop in first sc **and** in next ch-1 sp **and** in last sc, YO and draw through all 4 loops on hook; finish off.

*Design by Carol L. Jensen.*

# Friendship Rings

**INTERMEDIATE**

**Finished Size:** 4½" x 61" (11.5 cm x 155 cm) (before Lattice Trim)

## SHOPPING LIST

### Yarn (Medium Weight) MEDIUM 4

**[**2.5 ounces, 120 yards (70.9 grams, 109 meters) per skein**]**:

- ☐ Brown - 2 skeins

**[**2 ounces, 95 yards (56.7 grams, 86 meters) per skein**]**:

- ☐ Ombre - 2 skeins

### Crochet Hook

- ☐ Size I (5.5 mm) **or** size needed for gauge

### Additional Supplies

- ☐ Wooden beads - 10 (hole needs to be large enough to fit 2 strands of yarn)
- ☐ Yarn needle

## GAUGE INFORMATION

**Gauge Swatch:**

1¾" (4.5 cm) diameter

Work same as First Ring, page 56.

## STITCH GUIDE

**TREBLE CROCHET** *(abbreviated tr)*

YO twice, insert hook in st indicated, YO and pull up a loop (4 loops on hook), (YO and draw through 2 loops on hook) 3 times.

**PUFF ST** (uses one st or sp)

★ YO, insert hook in st or sp indicated, YO and pull up a loop even with loop on hook; repeat from ★ 3 times **more** (9 loops on hook), YO and draw through 8 loops on hook, YO and draw through remaining 2 loops on hook.

## FIRST RING

With Brown, ch 12; join with slip st to form a ring.

**Rnd 1** (Right side)**:** Ch 1, 26 sc in ring working over beginning yarn end; join with slip st to first sc, finish off.

*Note:* Loop a short piece of yarn around any stitch to mark Rnd 1 as **right** side and First Ring.

*Tip:* It is much easier to weave in yarn ends after you finish each Ring.

## NEXT 53 RINGS

Make rings, alternating Brown and Ombre.

*Tip:* It is very important that you link each new Ring to the **previous** Ring made. This is why the First Ring is marked. Also, hold the previous Ring with **right** side facing and insert the chain from **front** to **back**, so that they will all interlock in the same direction.

With next color, ch 12; insert ch through previous ring from **front** to **back** and join with slip st to form a ring.

**Rnd 1** (Right side)**:** Ch 1, 26 sc in ring working over beginning yarn end; join with slip st to first sc, finish off.

## EDGING

**Rnd 1:** With **right** side facing, join Ombre with sc in any sc on First Ring *(see Joining With Sc, page 91)*; sc in next 3 sc; ★ with **right** side of next Ring facing, hdc in any sc, sc in next 3 sc; repeat from ★ across (all rings interlock in the same direction); (ch 4, skip next 3 sc, sc in next 4 sc) twice, (skip next 9 sc on next Ring, hdc in next sc, sc in next 3 sc) across to last ring, skip next 8 sc on last Ring, hdc in next sc, sc in next 3 sc, ch 4, skip next 3 sc, sc in next 4 sc, ch 4, skip last 3 sc; join with slip st to first sc: 440 sts and 4 ch-4 sps.

**Rnd 2:** Ch 3 **(counts as first hdc plus ch 1, now and throughout)**, † (skip next st, hdc in next st, ch 1) across to within one sc of next corner ch-4 sp, skip next sc, hdc in next ch, ch 1, skip next ch, 2 hdc in next ch, ch 1, skip next ch, (hdc in next sc, ch 1, skip next sc) twice, hdc in next ch, ch 1, skip next ch, 2 hdc in next ch, ch 1, skip next ch †, hdc in next st, ch 1, repeat from † to † once; join with slip st to first hdc: 232 hdc and 228 ch-1 sps.

**Rnd 3:** Slip st in next ch, ch 3, ★ (skip next hdc, hdc in next ch, ch 1) across to next corner 2-hdc group, skip next hdc, 2 hdc in next hdc, ch 1, 2 hdc in next ch, ch 1, skip next hdc, (hdc in next ch, ch 1, skip next hdc) 3 times, 2 hdc in next hdc, ch 1, 2 hdc in next ch, ch 1; repeat from ★ once **more**; join with slip st to first hdc, finish off: 240 hdc and 232 ch-1 sps.

**Rnd 4:** With **right** side facing, join Brown with dc in next-to-the-last ch-1 sp made *(see Joining With Dc, page 91)*; dc in same sp, † ch 1, skip next hdc, work Puff St in next hdc, ch 1, (work Puff St in next ch-1 sp, ch 1) across to next corner 2-hdc group, skip next hdc, work Puff St in next hdc, ch 1, (2 dc, ch 1) twice in next ch-1 sp, skip next hdc, work Puff St in next hdc, ch 1, (work Puff St in next ch-1 sp, ch 1) 4 times, skip next hdc, work Puff St in next hdc, ch 1 †, (2 dc, ch 1, 2 dc) in next ch-1 sp, repeat from † to † once, 2 dc in same sp as first dc, sc in top of first dc made to form last ch-1 sp; do **not** finish off.

## LATTICE TRIM

### First Side

**Row 1:** Turn; slip st in first dc, ch 1, sc in same st and in each st and ch-1 sp across to next corner ch-1 sp: 17 sc.

**Row 2:** Ch 1, turn; sc in first sc, ★ ch 6, skip next 3 sc, sc in next sc; repeat from ★ across: 4 loops.

**Row 3:** Ch 8, turn; sc in first loop, (ch 6, sc in next loop) 3 times, ch 3, tr in last sc to form last loop.

**Row 4:** Ch 1, turn; sc in first tr, (ch 6, sc in next loop) 4 times.

**Row 5:** Ch 8, turn; sc in first loop, (ch 6, sc in next loop) 3 times, ch 3, tr in last sc to form last loop; finish off.

### Second Side

**Row 1:** With **wrong** side facing, join Brown with sc in dc after corner ch-1 sp; sc in next dc and in each st and ch-1 sp across to next corner ch-1 sp: 17 sc.

**Rows 2-5:** Work same as First Side.

## SMALL RING

Make 6 Brown and 4 Ombre.

Leaving a long end for joining ring, ch 6; join with slip st to form a ring.

**Rnd 1** (Right side)**:** Ch 1, 12 sc in ring; join with slip st to first sc, finish off leaving a long end for joining ring.

Thread a yarn needle with both ends and insert it through a bead. Attach a Small Ring to the center chain of each loop on last row of Lattice Trim in the following order: Place a Brown Ring on each end loop and on the center loop, and place an Ombre Ring in the loop between them.

*Design by Mary Estok Nolfi.*

# Classic Cable

**INTERMEDIATE**

**Finished Size:** 5" x 64" (12.5 cm x 162.5 cm)

## SHOPPING LIST ⟵

### Yarn (Medium Weight)

**[**2.5 ounces, 120 yards

(70.9 grams, 109 meters) per skein**]**:

- ☐ 4 skeins

### Crochet Hooks

- ☐ Size H (5 mm) **and**
- ☐ Size I (5.5 mm)

  **or** sizes needed for gauge

## GAUGE INFORMATION

Using larger size hook,

in Cable pattern,

18 sts = 5" (12.75 cm);

16 rows = 4" (10 cm)

**Gauge Swatch:**

3" (7.5 cm) square

Using larger size hook, ch 12.

**Row 1:** Sc in second ch from hook and in each ch across: 11 sc.

**Rows 2-12:** Ch 1, turn; sc in each sc across.

Finish off.

## STITCH GUIDE

### FRONT POST DOUBLE CROCHET

*(abbreviated FPdc)*

YO, working in **front** of previous row *(Fig. 5, page 93)*, insert hook from **front** to **back** around post of st indicated *(Fig. 4, page 93)*, YO and pull up a loop (3 loops on hook), (YO and draw through 2 loops on hook) twice.

## RIBBING

Using smaller size hook, ch 16.

**Row 1:** Sc in second ch from hook and in each ch across: 15 sc.

**Rows 2-18:** Ch 1, turn; sc in Back Loop Only of each sc across *(Fig. 1, page 92)*.

Do **not** finish off.

## CABLE PATTERN

Change to larger size hook.

**Row 1** (Right side)**:** Ch 1, sc in end of each row across Ribbing: 18 sc.

**Row 2 AND ALL WRONG SIDE ROWS:** Ch 1, turn; sc in both loops of each st across.

**Row 3:** Ch 1, turn; sc in first 2 sc, work FPdc around third sc on Row 1, skip sc behind FPdc, sc in next 4 sc, skip next 4 sc on Row 1, work FPdc around each of next 4 sc, skip 4 sc behind FPdc, sc in next 4 sc, skip next 4 sc on Row 1, work FPdc around next sc, skip sc behind FPdc, sc in last 2 sc.

**Row 5:** Ch 1, turn; sc in first 2 sc, work FPdc around next FPdc 2 rows **below**, skip sc behind FPdc, sc in next 4 sc, work FPdc around each of next 4 FPdc

2 rows **below**, skip 4 sc behind FPdc, sc in next 4 sc, work FPdc around next FPdc 2 rows **below**, skip sc behind FPdc, sc in last 2 sc.

**Row 7:** Ch 1, turn; sc in first 2 sc, work FPdc around next FPdc 2 rows **below**, skip sc behind FPdc, sc in next 3 sc, work FPdc around each of next 2 FPdc 2 rows **below**, skip 2 sc behind FPdc, sc in next 2 sc, work FPdc around each of next 2 FPdc 2 rows **below**, skip 2 sc behind FPdc, sc in next 3 sc, work FPdc around next FPdc 2 rows **below**, skip sc behind FPdc, sc in last 2 sc.

**Row 9:** Ch 1, turn; sc in first 2 sc, work FPdc around next FPdc 2 rows **below**, skip sc behind FPdc, sc in next 2 sc, work FPdc around each of next 2 FPdc 2 rows **below**, skip 2 sc behind FPdc, sc in next 4 sc, work FPdc around each of next 2 FPdc 2 rows **below**, skip 2 sc behind FPdc, sc in next 2 sc, work FPdc around next FPdc 2 rows **below**, skip sc behind FPdc, sc in last 2 sc.

**Row 11:** Repeat Row 9.

**Row 13:** Repeat Row 7.

**Row 15:** Repeat Row 5.

**Row 17:** Ch 1, turn; sc in first 2 sc, work FPdc around next FPdc 2 rows **below**, skip sc behind FPdc, sc in next 4 sc, skip next 2 FPdc 2 rows **below**, work FPdc around each of next 2 FPdc, working in **front** of last 2 FPdc made, work FPdc around each of 2 skipped FPdc, skip 4 sc behind FPdc, sc in next 4 sc, work FPdc around next FPdc 2 rows **below**, skip sc behind FPdc, sc in last 2 sc.

Repeat Rows 6-17 for pattern until piece measures approximately 58¼" (148 cm) from bottom of Ribbing, ending by working Row 13.

**Last 6 Rows:** Repeat Rows 4 and 5, 3 times.

Do **not** finish off.

## RIBBING

Change to smaller size hook.

**Row 1:** Ch 16, turn; sc in second ch from hook and in each ch across to last ch, pull up a loop in last ch, pull up a loop in first st on last row of Cable Pattern and draw through both loops on hook **(counts as last sc)**, slip st in next st, leave remaining sts unworked: 15 sc.

**Row 2:** Ch 1, turn; skip first slip st, sc in Back Loop Only of each sc across.

**Row 3:** Ch 1, turn; sc in Back Loop Only of first 14 sc, pull up a loop in Back Loop Only of next sc, pull up a loop in both loops of next st on last row of Cable Pattern and draw through both loops on hook **(counts as last sc)**, slip st in next st, leave remaining sts unworked: 15 sc.

**Rows 4-18:** Repeat Rows 2 and 3, 7 times; then repeat Row 2 once **more**.

Finish off.

*Design by Mary Estok Nolfi.*

# Zesty

EASY

**Finished Size:** 4½" x 60" (11.5 cm x 152.5 cm) (excluding fringe)

*Shown on page 65.*

## SHOPPING LIST ←

### Yarn (Medium Weight) MEDIUM 4

[3.5 ounces, 205 yards (100 grams, 187 meters) per skein]:

- ☐ White - 1 skein
- ☐ Teal - 30 yards (27.5 meters)
- ☐ Gold - 30 yards (27.5 meters)
- ☐ Pale Teal - 30 yards (27.5 meters)

### Crochet Hook

- ☐ Size H (5 mm) **or** size needed for gauge

## GAUGE INFORMATION

In pattern,

13 sts and 13 rows = 4" (10 cm)

**Gauge Swatch:** 4" wide x 3" high (10 cm x 7.5 cm)

With White, ch 14.

**Row 1:** Sc in second ch from hook and in each ch across: 13 sc.

**Rows 2 and 3:** Ch 1, turn; sc in each sc across.

**Row 4:** Ch 4 **(counts as first tr, now and throughout)**, turn; tr in next sc and in each sc across.

**Rows 5-7:** Ch 1, turn; sc in each st across.

**Row 8:** Ch 4, turn; tr in next sc and in each sc across; finish off.

## STITCH GUIDE

### TREBLE CROCHET

*(abbreviated tr)*

YO twice, insert hook in st indicated, YO and pull up a loop (4 loops on hook), (YO and draw through 2 loops on hook) 3 times.

When changing colors *(Fig. 3a, page 92)*, leave an 8" (20.5 cm) end of Teal, Gold or Pale Teal at each end of Rows 3, 7, and 11 to be added later to fringe.

## BODY

With White, ch 196.

**Row 1** (Right side)**:** Sc in second ch from hook and in each ch across: 195 sc.

*Note:* Loop a short piece of yarn around any stitch to mark Row 1 as **right** side.

**Row 2:** Ch 1, turn; sc in each sc across changing to Teal in last sc; cut White.

**Row 3:** Ch 1, turn; sc in first 2 sc, ch 7, ★ skip next 3 sc, sc in next sc, ch 7; repeat from ★ across to last 5 sc, skip next 3 sc, sc in last 2 sc changing to White in last sc; cut Teal: 51 sc and 48 ch-7 loops.

**Row 4:** Ch 3 **(counts as first dc)**, turn; dc in next sc, working in **front** of ch-7 loop *(Fig. 5, page 93)* and in skipped sc **below**, dc in next sc, tr in next sc, dc in next sc, ★ dc in next sc on previous row, working in **front** of ch-7 loop and in skipped sc **below**, dc in next sc, tr in next sc, dc in next sc; repeat from ★ across to last 2 sc on previous row, dc in last 2 sc: 195 sts.

**Row 5:** Ch 1, turn; sc in first 3 dc, working **around** next ch-7, sc in next tr, sc in next 3 dc, ★ working **around** next ch-7, sc in next tr, sc in next 3 dc; repeat from ★ across.

**Row 6:** Ch 1, turn; sc in each sc across changing to Gold in last sc; cut White.

**Row 7:** Ch 1, turn; sc in first 2 sc, ch 7, ★ skip next 3 sc, sc in next sc, ch 7; repeat from ★ across to last 5 sc, skip next 3 sc, sc in last 2 sc changing to White in last sc; cut Gold: 51 sc and 48 ch-7 loops.

**Rows 8 and 9:** Repeat Rows 4 and 5.

**Row 10:** Ch 1, turn; sc in each sc across changing to Pale Teal in last sc; cut White.

**Row 11:** Ch 1, turn; sc in first 2 sc, ch 7, ★ skip next 3 sc, sc in next sc, ch 7; repeat from ★ across to last 5 sc, skip next 3 sc, sc in last 2 sc changing to White in last sc; cut Pale Teal: 51 sc and 48 ch-7 loops.

**Rows 12 and 13:** Repeat Rows 4 and 5.

**Rows 14 and 15:** Ch 1, turn; sc in each sc across.

Finish off.

## First Side Trim

With **right** side facing, join White with slip st in first sc on Row 15; slip st loosely in each sc across; finish off.

## Second Side Trim

With **right** side facing and working in free loops of beginning ch *(Fig. 2, pag 92)*, join White with slip st in first ch; slip st loosely in each ch across; finish off.

## FRINGE

Holding six strands of corresponding color yarn together, each 10" (25.5 cm) long, add fringe to ends of Rows 3, 7, and 11 *(Figs. 7c & d, page 94)*.

*Design by Ruthie Marks.*

# Ruffles

EASY

**Finished Size:** Approximately 4½" x 44" (11.5 cm x 112 cm) relaxed

## SHOPPING LIST ←

### Yarn (Mesh Super Bulky Weight) SUPER BULKY 6

[3.5 ounces, 30 yards (100 grams, 27 meters) per ball]:

- ☐ 1 ball

### Crochet Hook

- ☐ Size H (5 mm)

### Additional Supplies

- ☐ Sewing needle and matching thread
- ☐ Split-ring markers

---

Gauge is not important for this project.

*Tip:* To prevent the piece from accidentally unraveling when you are not working on your project, slip the loop from your hook onto a safety pin.

## TECHNIQUES USED

### SC USING 4 LOOPS

Insert your hook in the next stitch on your project, skip the next loop on the yarn, insert your hook in the next loop and pull the loop through the stitch *(Fig. A)* (2 loops on hook).

**Fig. A**

Skip the next loop on the yarn, insert your hook in the next loop and pull the loop through both loops on the hook *(Fig. B)*.

**Fig. B**

## SCARF

When working a Foundation Chain, place a marker in the first chain made *(Fig. C or D)*. It may be helpful to also place a marker in each chain as it is made. This will help you see where to insert your hook on Row 1 *(Fig. E)*.

**Fig. C**

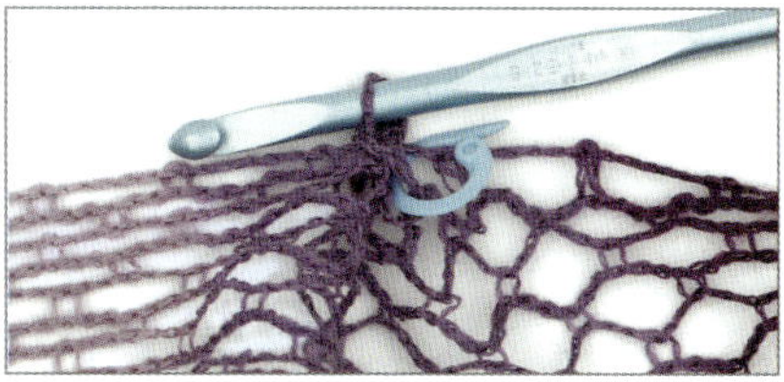

**Fig. D**

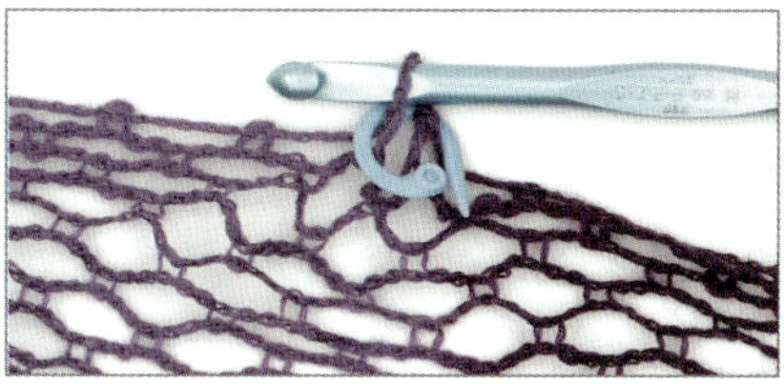

**Fig. E**

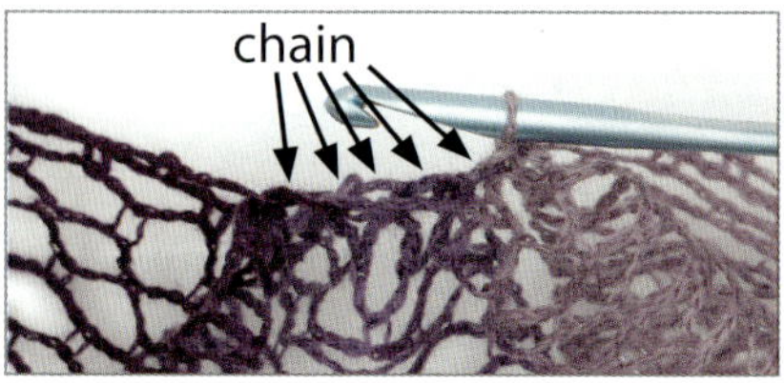


As you work, stretch the yarn out, having the mesh edge at the top. Work only in the top row of mesh loops.

**Foundation Chain:** Skip first 8 loops from end and insert hook in next loop, (skip next loop, ch 1) 5 times: 5 chs.

Work all sc using 4 loops *(Figs. A and B, page 71)*.

Remove marker as you work into the marked stitch.

**Row 1:** Turn; skip first ch, sc in next ch, place marker in sc just made, sc in last 3 chs: 4 sc.

**Row 2:** Ch 1, turn; skip turning ch just made, sc in next sc, place marker in sc just made, sc in last 3 sc.

Repeat Row 2 until there are at least 8 top loops remaining on the mesh yarn after completing a row.

Trim the mesh yarn leaving 8 loops.

To secure the loop on your hook, carefully slip the loop off your hook and using a sewing needle and matching thread, sew the loop in place ***(Fig. F)***.

**Fig. F**

Hide the raw edge of the yarn using one of the following methods:

The top edge of the end can be gathered or it can be folded twice to the inside; the corner can be folded up; or the short end can be tucked under the last ruffle. Using a sewing needle and matching thread, sew the end in place.

You can also use a large yarn needle and weave the ends into the ruffle.

*Design by Lisa Gentry.*

# Great Outdoors Hoodie

EASY

**Finished Scarf Measurement:** 6" x 69" (15 cm x 175.5 cm)
(excluding fringe loops)

**Finished Hood Size:** One size fits most Adults

## SHOPPING LIST ⟵

### Yarn (Medium Weight) 4

[5 ounces, 236 yards (141 grams, 215 meters) per skein]:

- ☐ 2 skeins

### Crochet Hook

- ☐ Size H (5 mm) **or** size needed for gauge

## GAUGE INFORMATION

In pattern, 14 sts = 4" (10 cm);
9 rows = 3¼" (8.25 cm)

**Gauge Swatch:**
4¼" wide x 3¼" high
(10.75 cm x 8.25 cm)

Ch 16.

**Row 1:** Sc in second ch from hook and in each ch across: 15 sc.

**Row 2:** Ch 1, turn; sc in Back Loop Only of each sc across *(Fig. 1, page 92)*.

**Row 3:** Ch 4 **(counts as first dc plus ch 1)**, turn; skip next sc, dc in Back Loop Only of next sc, ★ ch 1, skip next sc, dc in Back Loop Only of next sc; repeat from ★ across: 8 dc and 7 chs.

**Row 4:** Ch 1, turn; sc in Back Loop Only of first dc, (sc in next ch, sc in Back Loop Only of next dc) across: 15 sts.

**Rows 5-9:** Repeat Rows 2-4 once, then repeat Rows 2 and 3 once **more**.

Finish off.

## STITCH GUIDE

**SINGLE CROCHET 2 TOGETHER**

***(abbreviated sc2tog)***

Pull up a loop in each of next 2 sc, YO and draw through all 3 loops on hook.

## SCARF

Ch 281.

**Row 1:** Sc in 41st ch from hook **(fringe loop made)** and in each ch across: 241 sc.

**Row 2** (Right side)**:** Ch 40 **(fringe loop made, now and throughout)**, turn; sc in Back Loop Only of each sc across *(Fig. 1, page 92)*.

*Note:* Loop a short piece of yarn around any stitch to mark Row 2 as **right** side.

**Row 3:** Ch 40, turn; dc in Back Loop Only of first sc, ★ ch 1, skip next sc, dc in Back Loop Only of next sc; repeat from ★ across: 121 dc and 120 chs.

**Row 4:** Ch 40, turn; sc in Back Loop Only of first dc, (sc in next ch, sc in Back Loop Only of next dc) across: 241 sc.

**Row 5:** Ch 40, turn; sc in Back Loop Only of each sc across.

**Rows 6-17:** Repeat Rows 3-5, 4 times.

Finish off.

## HOOD

**Row 1:** With **right** side facing, skip first 80 sc and join yarn with dc in Back Loop Only of next sc *(see Joining With Dc, page 91)*; ★ ch 1, skip next sc, dc in Back Loop Only of next sc; repeat from ★ 39 times **more**, leave remaining 80 sc unworked: 41 dc and 40 chs.

**Row 2:** Ch 1, turn; sc in Back Loop Only of first sc, (sc in next ch, sc in Back Loop Only of next sc) across: 81 sc.

**Row 3:** Ch 1, turn; sc in Back Loop Only of each sc across.

**Row 4:** Ch 4 **(counts as first dc plus ch 1)**, turn; skip next sc, dc in Back Loop Only of next sc, ★ ch 1, skip next sc, dc in Back Loop Only of next sc; repeat from ★ across: 41 dc and 40 chs.

**Rows 5-9:** Repeat Rows 2-4 once, then repeat Rows 2 and 3 once **more**: 81 sc.

**Joining Row** (Back Hook seam)**:** Ch 1, turn; with **right** side together, matching sts on Row 9, and working through **outside** loops of **both** thicknesses, sc in first 34 sc, sc2tog 3 times; finish off.

*Design by Barbara Shaffer.*

# Glitzy Cowl

**EASY**

**Finished Size:** 6½" wide x 32" long (16.5 cm x 81.5 cm)

## SHOPPING LIST ←

### Yarn (Medium Weight) MEDIUM 4

[3.5 ounces, 202 yards (100 grams, 185 meters) per skein]:

- ☐ 1 skein

### Crochet Hook

- ☐ Size H (5 mm) **or** size needed for gauge

### Additional Supplies

- ☐ 7/8" (22 mm) Buttons - 3
- ☐ Sewing needle and matching thread

---

## GAUGE INFORMATION

In pattern, (dc, ch 1, dc) 3 times = 2" (5 cm); 6 rows = 2¾" (7 cm)

**Gauge Swatch:**

5¾" wide x 2¾" high (14.5 cm x 7 cm)

Work same as Body, page 80, for 6 rows: 18 dc and 8 ch-1 sps.

## STITCH GUIDE

### PICOT

Ch 3, slip st in third ch from hook.

## BODY

Ch 28.

**Row 1** (Right side)**:** (Dc, ch 1, dc) in fifth ch from hook **(4 skipped chs count as first dc plus one skipped ch)**, ★ skip next 2 chs, (dc, ch 1, dc) in next ch; repeat from ★ across to last 2 chs, skip next ch, dc in last ch: 18 dc and 8 ch-1 sps.

*Note:* Loop a short piece of yarn around any stitch to mark Row 1 as **right** side.

**Row 2:** Ch 3 **(counts as first dc)**, turn; (dc, ch 1, dc) in each ch-1 sp across to last 2 dc, skip next dc, dc in last dc.

Repeat Row 2 until piece measures approximately 30" (76 cm) from beginning ch, ending by working a **wrong** side row; do **not** finish off.

## EDGING

**Rnd 1:** Ch 4 **(counts as first dc plus ch 1)**, turn; (dc, ch 1) twice in first dc, (dc in next ch-1 sp, ch 1) across to last 2 dc, skip next dc, (dc, ch 1) 3 times in last dc; working in ends of rows, dc in first row, ch 1, (dc in next row, ch 1) across; working in free loops of beginning ch *(Fig. 2, page 92)*, (dc, ch 1) 3 times in first ch, skip next ch, dc in next ch, ch 1, (skip next 2 chs, dc in next ch, ch 1) 7 times, skip next ch, (dc, ch 1) 3 times in next ch; working in ends of rows, dc in first row, ch 1, (dc in next row, ch 1) across; join with slip st to first dc.

**Rnd 2:** (Slip st, ch 1, sc, work Picot, sc) in next ch-1 sp, (sc, work Picot, sc) in next ch-1 sp and in each ch-1 sp around; join with slip st to first sc, finish off.

Using photo as a guide for placement, sew buttons evenly spaced across bottom edge.

To wear your Cowl as shown above, use ch-1 sps on Rnd 1 of Edging as buttonholes.

To wear your Cowl as shown on page 78, use ch-1 sps on Rnd 1 of Edging formed at the side edge as buttonholes.

*Design by Melissa Leapman.*

# Hillcrest

EASY

**Finished Size:** 6" x 68½" (15 cm x 174 cm)

## SHOPPING LIST

### Yarn (Bulky Weight) BULKY 5

[3.5 ounces, 120 yards (100 grams, 109 meters) per skein]:

- ☐ Lt Blue - 1 skein
- ☐ Green - 1 skein

### Crochet Hook

- ☐ Size M/N (9 mm) **or** size needed for gauge

## GAUGE INFORMATION

In pattern, 12 sc = 5¾" (14.5 cm); Rows 1-3 = 3" (7.5 cm)

**Gauge Swatch:** 8⅛"w x 3"h (20.5 cm x 7.5 cm)

With Lt Blue, ch 18.

Work same as First Half, page 84: 16 sts and 5 ch-1 sps.

## FIRST HALF

With Lt Blue, ch 144; place marker in second ch from hook for Second Half placement.

**Row 1** (Right side)**:** Sc in second ch from hook and in each ch across: 143 sc.

*Note:* Loop a short piece of yarn around any stitch to mark Row 1 as **right** side.

**Row 2:** Ch 3 **(counts as first dc, now and throughout)**, turn; 3 dc in next sc, ★ ch 2, skip next 6 sc, (3 dc, ch 1, 3 dc) in next sc; repeat from ★ across to last 8 sc, ch 2, skip next 6 sc, 3 dc in next sc, dc in last sc: 122 dc and 39 sps.

**Row 3:** Ch 3, turn; 3 dc in next dc, ch 1, slip st in next ch-2 sp, ch 1, ★ (3 dc, ch 1) twice in next ch-1 sp, slip st in next ch-2 sp, ch 1; repeat from ★ across to last 4 dc, skip next 2 dc, 3 dc in next dc, dc in last dc; finish off.

## SECOND HALF

**Row 1:** With **right** side facing and working in free loops of beginning ch *(Fig. 2, page 92)*, join Green with sc in first ch *(see Joining With Sc, page 91)*; sc in next ch and in each ch across ending in marked ch, remove marker: 143 sc.

**Rows 2 and 3:** Repeat Rows 2 and 3 of First Half.

*Design by Ruthie Marks.*

# Button-Up Cowl

EASY

**Finished Size:** 7" high x 28" long (18 cm x 71 cm)

*Shown on page 85.*

## SHOPPING LIST

### Yarn (Medium Weight) MEDIUM 4

[3.5 ounces, 170 yards (100 grams, 156 meters) per skein]:

- ☐ 1 skein

### Crochet Hook

- ☐ Size I (5.5 mm) **or** size needed for gauge

### Additional Supplies

- ☐ 1$^3/_8$" (35 mm) Buttons - 3
- ☐ Sewing needle and matching thread

## GAUGE INFORMATION

In pattern,

2 repeats = 4½" (11.5 cm)

**Gauge Swatch:**

7" wide x 4½" high (17.75 cm x 11.5 cm)

Work same as Cowl for 8 rows: 28 dc and 3 sc.

## COWL

Ch 23.

**Row 1:** Sc in second ch from hook and in next 2 chs, ★ ch 3, skip next 2 chs, sc in next 5 chs; repeat from ★ once **more**, ch 3, skip next 2 chs, sc in last 3 chs: 16 sc and 3 ch-3 sps.

**Row 2** (Right side)**:** Ch 1, turn; sc in first sc, ★ 9 dc in next ch-3 sp, skip next 2 sc, sc in next sc; repeat from ★ 2 times **more**: 27 dc and 4 sc.

***Note:*** Loop a short piece of yarn around any stitch to mark Row 2 as **right** side.

**Row 3:** Ch 4 **(counts as first dc plus ch 1)**, turn; skip next 2 dc, sc in next 5 dc, ★ ch 3, skip next 5 sts, sc in next 5 dc; repeat from ★ once **more**, ch 1, skip next 2 dc, dc in last sc: 17 sts and 4 sps.

**Row 4:** Ch 3 **(counts as first dc)**, turn; 4 dc in first dc, skip next 2 sc, sc in next sc, ★ 9 dc in next ch-3 sp, skip next 2 sc, sc in next sc; repeat from ★ once **more**, skip next 2 sc and last ch-1 sp, 5 dc in last dc: 28 dc and 3 sc.

**Row 5:** Ch 1, turn; sc in first 3 dc, ★ ch 3, skip next 5 sts, sc in next 5 dc; repeat from ★ once **more**, ch 3, skip next 5 sts, sc in last 3 dc: 16 sc and 3 ch-3 sps.

**Row 6:** Ch 1, turn; sc in first sc, ★ 9 dc in next ch-3 sp, skip next 2 sc, sc in next sc; repeat from ★ 2 times **more**: 27 dc and 4 sc.

Repeat Rows 3-6 for pattern until piece measures approximately 27" (68.5 cm) from beginning ch, ending by working Row 4.

**Last Row:** Ch 1, turn; sc in first 3 dc, ★ ch 2, skip next 5 sts, sc in next 5 dc; repeat from ★ once **more**, ch 2, skip next 5 sts, sc in last 3 dc: 16 sc and 3 ch-2 sps.

**Trim:** Ch 1, turn; 3 sc in first sc, sc in next 2 sc, 2 sc in next ch-2 sp, (sc in next 5 sc, 2 sc in next ch-2 sp) twice, sc in next 2 sc, 3 sc in last sc; sc evenly across ends of rows; working in free loops of beginning ch *(Fig. 2, page 92)*, 3 sc in ch at base of first sc, sc in next 2 chs, 2 sc in next ch-2 sp, (sc in next 5 chs, 2 sc in next ch-2 sp) twice, sc in next 2 chs, 3 sc in last ch; sc evenly across ends of rows; join with slip st to first sc, finish off.

With **right** side facing and using photo as a guide for placement, sew one button at base of each 9-dc group on Row 2.

To wear your Cowl as shown above, use ch-2 sps on last row as buttonholes.

To wear your Cowl as shown on page 85, use spaces formed at the side edge as buttonholes.

# General Instructions

## ABBREVIATIONS

| | |
|---|---|
| BPdc | Back Post double crochet(s) |
| ch(s) | chain(s) |
| cm | centimeters |
| dc | double crochet(s) |
| dc2tog | double crochet 2 together |
| FPdc | Front Post double crochet(s) |
| hdc | half double crochet(s) |
| lqtr | linked quadruple treble crochet(s) |
| mm | millimeters |
| Rnd(s) | Round(s) |
| sc | single crochet(s) |
| sc2tog | single crochet 2 together |
| sp(s) | space(s) |
| st(s) | stitch(es) |
| tr | treble crochet(s) |
| YO | yarn over |

## SYMBOLS & TERMS

★ — work instructions following ★ as many **more** times as indicated in addition to the first time.

† to † — work all instructions from first † to second † **as many** times as specified.

( ) or **[ ]** — work enclosed instructions **as many** times as specified by the number immediately following **or** work all enclosed instructions in the stitch or space indicated **or** contains explanatory remarks.

colon (:) — the number(s) given after a colon at the end of a row or round denote(s) the number of stitches or spaces you should have on that row or round.

| CROCHET HOOKS | | | | | | | | | | | | | | | | | |
|---|---|---|---|---|---|---|---|---|---|---|---|---|---|---|---|---|---|
| **U.S.** | B-1 | C-2 | D-3 | E-4 | F-5 | G-6 | 7 | H-8 | I-9 | J-10 | K-10½ | L-11 | M/N-13 | N/P-15 | P/Q | Q | S |
| **Metric - mm** | 2.25 | 2.75 | 3.25 | 3.5 | 3.75 | 4 | 4.5 | 5 | 5.5 | 6 | 6.5 | 8 | 9 | 10 | 15 | 16 | 19 |

| CROCHET TERMINOLOGY | | |
|---|---|---|
| UNITED STATES | | INTERNATIONAL |
| slip stitch (slip st) | = | single crochet (sc) |
| single crochet (sc) | = | double crochet (dc) |
| half double crochet (hdc) | = | half treble crochet (htr) |
| double crochet (dc) | = | treble crochet (tr) |
| treble crochet (tr) | = | double treble crochet (dtr) |
| double treble crochet (dtr) | = | triple treble crochet (ttr) |
| triple treble crochet (tr tr) | = | quadruple treble crochet (qtr) |
| skip | = | miss |

| | |
|---|---|
| **BEGINNER** | Projects for first-time crocheters using basic stitches. Minimal shaping. |
| **EASY** | Projects using yarn with basic stitches, repetitive stitch patterns, simple color changes, and simple shaping and finishing. |
| **INTERMEDIATE** | Projects using a variety of techniques, such as basic lace patterns or color patterns, mid-level shaping and finishing. |
| **EXPERIENCED** | Projects with intricate stitch patterns, techniques and dimension, such as non-repeating patterns, multi-color techniques, fine threads, small hooks, detailed shaping and refined finishing. |

| Yarn Weight Symbol & Names | LACE 0 | SUPER FINE 1 | FINE 2 | LIGHT 3 | MEDIUM 4 | BULKY 5 | SUPER BULKY 6 | JUMBO 7 |
|---|---|---|---|---|---|---|---|---|
| Type of Yarns in Category | Fingering, size 10 crochet thread | Sock, Fingering, Baby | Sport, Baby | DK, Light Worsted | Worsted, Afghan, Aran | Chunky, Craft, Rug | Super Bulky, Roving | Jumbo, Roving |
| Crochet Gauge* Ranges in Single Crochet to 4" (10 cm) | 32-42 sts** | 21-32 sts | 16-20 sts | 12-17 sts | 11-14 sts | 8-11 sts | 6-9 sts | 5 sts and fewer |
| Advised Hook Size Range | Steel*** 6 to 8, Regular hook B-1 | B-1 to E-4 | E-4 to 7 | 7 to I-9 | I-9 to K-10½ | K-10½ to M/N-13 | M/N-13 to Q | Q and larger |

*GUIDELINES ONLY: The chart above reflects the most commonly used gauges and hook sizes for specific yarn categories.

** Lace weight yarns are usually crocheted with larger hooks to create lacy openwork patterns. Accordingly, a gauge range is difficult to determine. Always follow the gauge stated in your pattern.

*** Steel crochet hooks are sized differently from regular hooks–the higher the number, the smaller the hook, which is the reverse of regular hook sizing.

## GAUGE

Exact gauge is essential for proper size. Before beginning your project, make the sample swatch given in the individual instructions in the yarn and hook specified. After completing the swatch, measure it, counting your stitches and rows carefully. If your swatch is larger or smaller than specified, **make another, changing hook size to get the correct gauge**. Keep trying until you find the size hook that will give you the specified gauge.

## MARKERS

Markers are used to help distinguish the beginning of each round being worked. Place a 2" (5 cm) scrap piece of yarn before the first stitch of each round, moving the marker after each round is complete.

## JOINING WITH SC

When instructed to join with sc, begin with a slip knot on the hook. Insert the hook in the stitch or space indicated, YO and pull up a loop, YO and draw through both loops on hook.

## JOINING WITH DC

When instructed to join with dc, begin with a slip knot on the hook. YO, holding loop on hook, insert hook in stitch or space indicated, YO and pull up a loop (3 loops on hook), (YO and draw through 2 loops on hook) twice.

## BACK OR FRONT LOOPS ONLY

Work only in loop(s) indicated by arrow *(Fig. 1)*.

**Fig. 1**

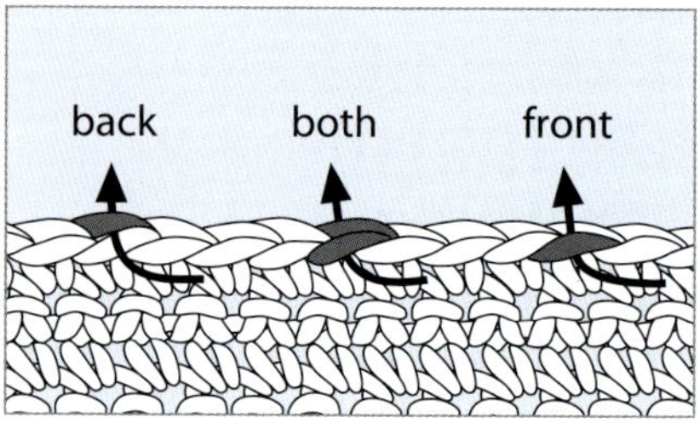


## FREE LOOPS OF A CHAIN

When instructed to work in free loops of a chain, work in loop indicated by arrow *(Fig. 2)*.

**Fig. 2**

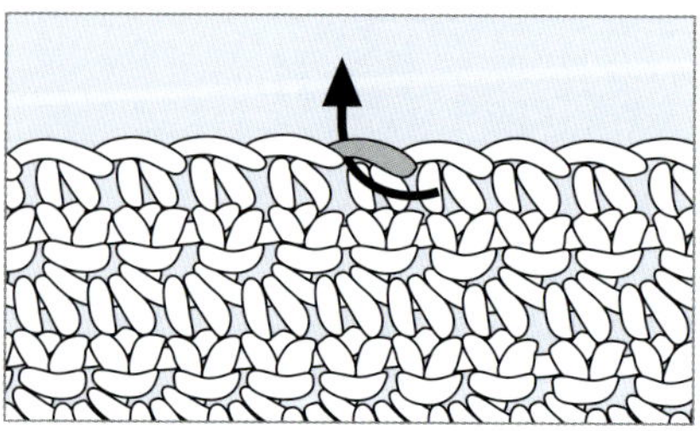

## CHANGING COLORS

Work the last stitch to within one step of completion, hook new yarn *(Figs. 3a, 3b or 3c)* and draw through both loops on hook.

**Fig. 3a**

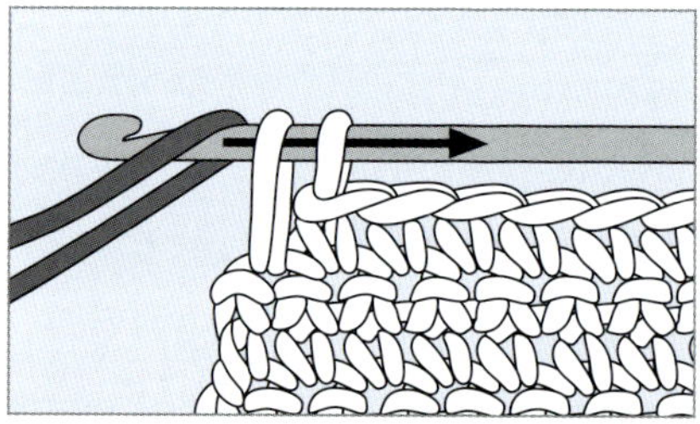

**Fig. 3b**

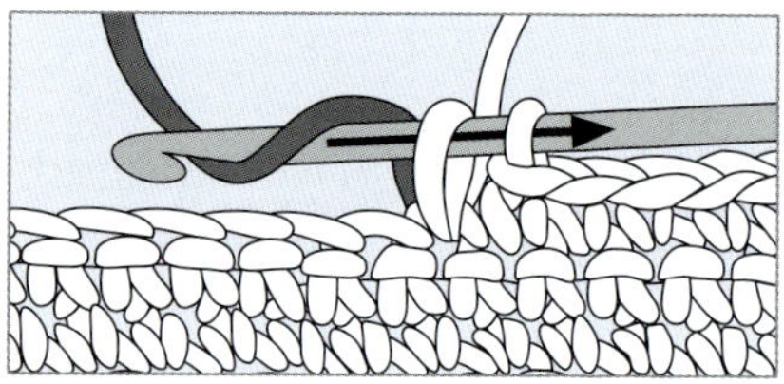

**Fig. 3c**

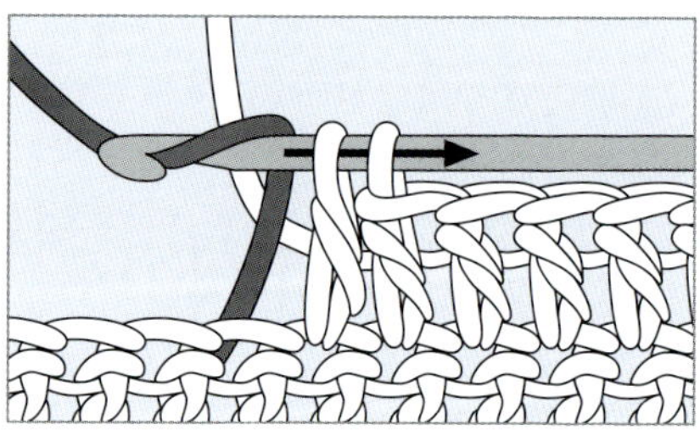

## POST STITCH

Work around post of stitch indicated, inserting hook in direction of arrow *(Fig. 4)*.

**Fig. 4**

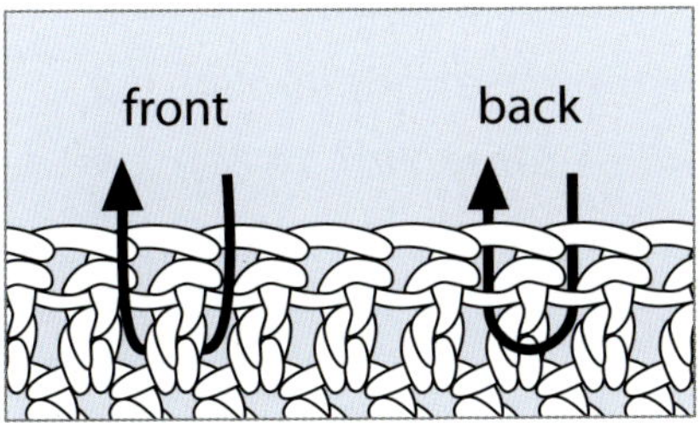


## WORKING IN FRONT OF OR AROUND A STITCH

Work in stitch or space indicated, inserting hook in direction of arrow *(Fig. 5)*.

**Fig. 5**

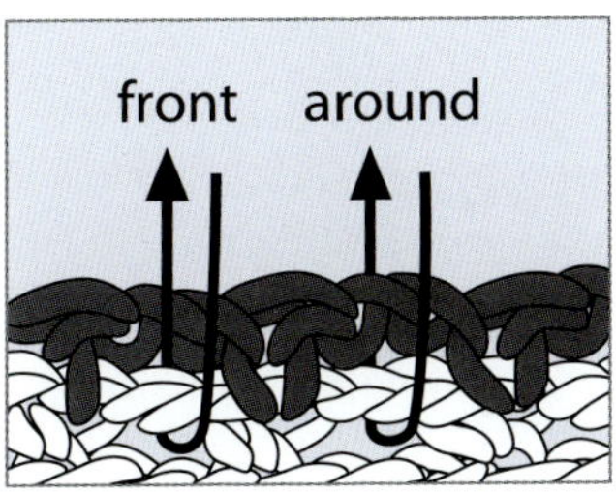


## WEAVE THROUGH STITCHES

Thread a yarn needle with the long end left at the end of a piece and weave it through the stitches on the last round worked *(Fig. 6)*.

**Fig. 6**

## FRINGE

Cut a piece of cardboard 3" (7.5 cm) wide and 5" (12.5 cm) long. Wind the yarn **loosely** and **evenly** lengthwise around the cardboard until the card is filled, then cut across one end; repeat as needed.

Hold together as many strands as specified in individual instructions; fold in half.

With **wrong** side facing and using a crochet hook, draw the folded end up through a stitch or row and pull the loose ends through the folded end ***(Figs. 7a & c)***; draw the knot up **tightly** ***(Figs. 7b & d)***.

Repeat, spacing as specified in individual instructions.

Lay flat on a hard surface and trim the ends.

**Fig. 7a**

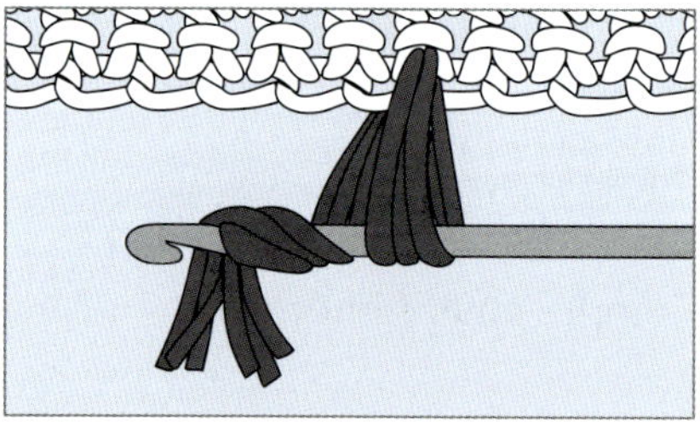

**Fig. 7b**

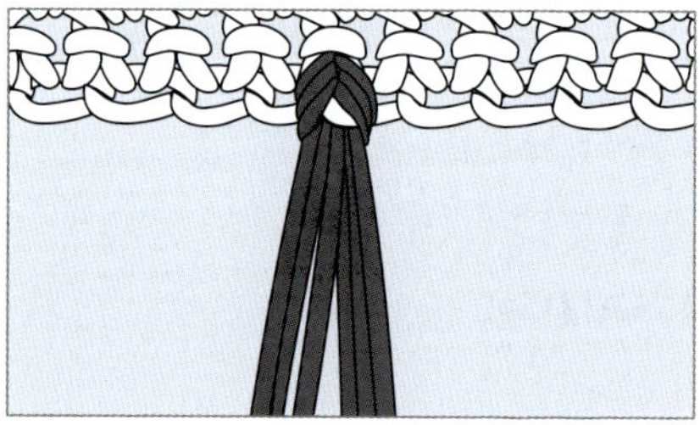

**Fig. 7c**

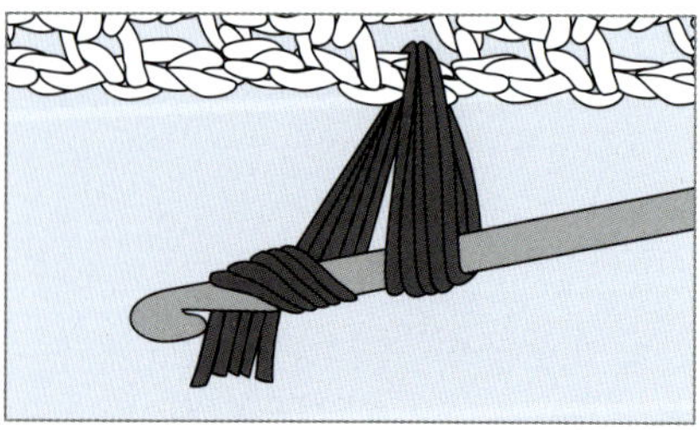

**Fig. 7d**

# Yarn Information

The Scarves in this book were made using a variety of yarn weights. Any brand of the specified weight of yarn may be used. It is best to refer to the yardage/meters when determining how many balls or skeins to purchase. Remember, to arrive at the finished size, it is the GAUGE/TENSION that is important, not the brand of yarn.

For your convenience, listed below are the specific yarns and colors used to create our photography models. Because yarn manufacturers make frequent changes in their product lines, you may sometimes find it necessary to use a substitute yarn or to search for the discontinued product at alternate suppliers (locally or online).

**INTUITIVE**
***Patons® Lace™***
#33046 Patina

**MARITIME**
***Lion Brand® Heartland®***
#113 Redwood

**ROUNDABOUT**
***Lion Brand® Vanna's Choice®***
Bright Purple - #145 Eggplant
Blue - #109 Colonial Blue
Lt Blue - #105 Silver Blue
Purple - #147 Purple

**PARKWAY**
***Red Heart® Medley™***
#930 Garden

**BASKETWEAVE**
***Lion Brand® Cotton-Ease®***
Brown - #122 Taupe
Dk Grey - #152 Charcoal
Cream - #099 Almond

**CONFIDENCE**
***Lion Brand® Vanna's Choice® Baby***
#114 Cheery Cherry

**DYNAMIC**
***Patons® Canadiana™***
Orange - #10630 Burnt Orange
Gold - #10610 Fool's Gold
Burgundy - #10430 Burgundy

**SIMPLICITY**
*Lily® Sugar 'n Cream®*
#00222 Butter Cream Ombre

**FILIGREE**
*Bernat® Softee® Chunky™*
#28008 Natural

**CHECKMATE**
*Lion Brand® Vanna's Choice®*
Purple - #147 Purple
Lt Purple - #146 Dusty Purple

**COLLEGIATE**
*Patons® Silk Bamboo™*
Plum - #85430 Plum
Gold - #85607 Saffron

**KEYHOLE ASCOT**
*Red Heart® Boutique Eclipse™*
#9851 Tidal Wave

**FRIENDSHIP RINGS**
*Lily® Sugar 'n Cream®*
Brown - #01011 Softly Taupe
Ombre - #02510 Rosewood

**CLASSIC CABLE**
*Lily® Sugar 'n Cream®*
#01725 Blueberry

**ZESTY**
*Patons® Canadiana™*
White - #10006 Winter White
Teal - #10744 Medium Teal
Gold - #10610 Fool's Gold
Pale Teal - #10743 Pale Teal

**RUFFLES**
*Red Heart® Boutique Sashay®*
#1946 Ballet

**GREAT OUTDOORS HOODIE**
*Red Heart® Super Saver®*
#971 Camouflage

**GLITZY COWL**
*Red Heart® Boutique Swanky™*
#9401 Sterling

**HILLCREST**
*Bernat® Roving™*
Lt Blue - #00098 Low Tide
Green - #00222 Clover

**BUTTON-UP COWL**
*Lion Brand® Vanna's Choice®*
#141 Wild Berry